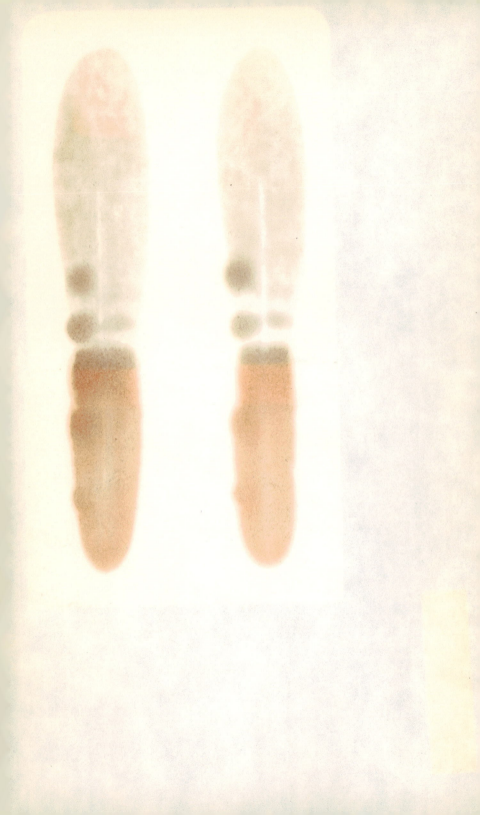

Twayne's Music Series

Chris Frigon and Camille Roman,
Consulting Editors

SONNY ROLLINS:

The Journey of a Jazzman

*Photograph of Sonny Rollins
by Charles Stewart*

SONNY ROLLINS:

The Journey of a Jazzman

Charles Blancq

Twayne Publishers

Sonny Rollins: The Journey of a Jazzman

Twayne's Music Series
Chris Frigon and Camille Roman,
Consulting Editors

Copyright © 1983 by G. K. Hall & Co.
All rights reserved

Published in 1983 by Twayne Publishers,
A Division of G. K. Hall & Co.
70 Lincoln Street, Boston, Mass. 02111

Printed on permanent/durable
acid-free paper and bound in
the United States of America

First Printing

Book design and production
by Barbara Anderson

Typeset in 10 pt. Zapf Book by Compset, Inc.,
with display type provided by Solotype.

**Library of Congress Cataloging in
Publication Data**

Blancq, Charles, 1940—
Sonny Rollins, the journey of a jazzman.

Bibliography: p. 119
Discography: p. 130
Includes index.
1. Rollins, Sonny.   2. Jazz
musicians—United States—
Biography   I. Title.
ML419.R64B6   1983   785.42'092'4   [B]
82-15860
ISBN 0-8057-9460-3

Contents

About the Author

Charles Blancq is a musicologist whose longtime interest in jazz led him to analytical studies of the music. Born in New Orleans in 1940, Blancq pursued a dual career as a jazz and symphonic musician before beginning graduate studies at North Texas State University in 1963. While at that institution, he was a student in musicology and composition of Cecil Adkins, Samuel Adler, Merrill Ellis, and the late Lloyd Hibberd. Graduate studies continued at Tulane University, from which he received the Ph.D. in Historical Musicology.

As a performing musician, Blancq has been active in both European music and jazz: He was a member of the New Orleans Philharmonic Symphony Orchestra (1959—1963); performed with the New Orleans Opera Orchestra under Renato Cellini, the Dallas Symphony Orchestra (1964—1965) under Donald Johanos, and has appeared with numerous jazz groups in New Orleans and elsewhere since he was a teenager.

Blancq is currently an Assistant Professor of Music at the University of New Orleans, having joined the music faculty in the fall of 1970. He teaches jazz history and improvisation courses, is a staff producer/host for WWNO-FM (National Public Radio affiliate in New Orleans), and directs the university jazz band.

Preface

Sonny Rollins pursues what must be one of the most bizarre careers of any living jazz musician. From a childhood in Harlem where he grew up in company with many of the pioneering jazzmen of the 1930s and 1940s, Rollins moved rapidly through the ranks with such casual ease, and at times such independence, that he must be regarded as a true "survivor" in the history of modern jazz. His precocious talent took him through virtually all of the post-World War II styles: bebop, post-bop, the avant-garde, and the eclectic pop/jazz movement of the 1970s. Consequently, *Sonny Rollins: The Journey of a Jazzman* is more than just a book about an outstanding jazz musician; it is an account of modern jazz itself: how it works, what are its essential ingredients, and how the listener can better grasp its musical content.

Understanding the contributions of a performer such as Rollins presumes a knowledge of jazz improvisation and how the process takes place. Therefore, a considerable effort is made to introduce the reader to the basic components of the music: its forms, procedures, rhythmic peculiarities, and especially the melodic aspect of improvisation. The performers, after all, were attempting to play melody, and although faced with the difficult task of having to create it spontaneously, all strove to make melodic sense out of what they improvised. Most writings on jazz, even those that are otherwise excellent, avoid discussion of this most important topic, preferring to concentrate instead on the music's historical or sociological implications or its legendry and origins. While entertaining and sometimes informative, they reveal little about the melody, rhythm, harmony, and form of jazz, and even less about its most mysterious ingredient: melodic improvisation.

The three pioneering studies that first analyzed the musical content of jazz are Winthrop Sargent's *Jazz Hot and Hybrid* (1946), Leonard Feather's *Inside Bebop* (1949), and André Hodeir's *Jazz: Its Evolution and Essence* (1956). Some years later these were followed by Gunther Schuller's *Early Jazz* (1968—the first truly modern study of the music) and Frank Tirro's *Jazz: A History* (1977—perhaps the best comprehensive one-volume survey of jazz to date)—not many sources when one considers the massive amount of music included under the general heading of jazz. In the interim, the popular American trade journals *Downbeat* and *Metronome,* and the English *Jazz Journal,* carried the bulk of writings about jazz; but here the emphasis was usually on record reviews or biography and only recently have there been consistent attempts at analyses of the music.

That the nature of jazz improvisation was not the subject of more investigations over the years is to a large extent due to the performers themselves, the majority of whom concentrated on playing the music and were unconcerned about the analysis of their performances. Whereas the classical performer is accustomed to a sophisticated theoretical analysis of his music, the jazz performer traditionally resisted such attempts to scrutinize his playing, sometimes viewing these efforts as contrived rationalizations of what for him was largely a matter of intuition. This is not to say that the traditional analytical procedures long applied to the study of European music are not applicable to the study of jazz, but only that they must be carefully applied and not be arbitrarily imposed. Jazz is perhaps best understood from the perspective of the creators themselves, and it is from this point of view that the most meaningful conclusions can be drawn about the music.

Many years of listening to jazz and following its musical developments have led to some observations fundamental to the inception of this study: that improvisation is an integral element of jazz; that this improvisation is essentially melodic; and that it underwent some significant conceptual development in the work of tenor saxophonist Theodore "Sonny" Rollins. Rollins, for a substantial portion of his career, was unique among jazzmen. He was a "thematic" improviser who based his improvisations on the theme of the tune rather than merely the chord changes and possessed a remarkable sense of formal logic, melodic, and rhythmic coherence in creating his melodic lines.

In preparation for this study, over three hundred performances of Sonny Rollins were analyzed through repeated listenings of recordings. Thirty-one of what I consider to be his most outstanding performances were transcribed into musical notation in order to permit closer examination and analysis. For points of comparison as well as perspective, this same procedure was applied to the recordings of other important jazz artists including Louis Armstrong, Coleman Hawkins, Miles Davis, Dizzy Gillespie, Bill Evans, Paul Desmond, Charlie Parker, John Coltrane, and Lester Young. In the absence of other documentation, phonograph recordings, by necessity, form the most important source of information concerning Rollins's music. The reader, therefore, will gain the maximum understanding of the matters under discussion by listening to the recordings; no amount of analysis or explanation can substitute for the clarification that they provide.

Since scholarly studies on jazz topics are a relatively new phenomenom, the support of friends and colleagues has been particularly invaluable to me in seeing this project through. I am greatly indebted to Professor Peter Hansen of Tulane University, who in 1969 first encouraged me to investigate the study of jazz, and to Dick Allen and Curtis Jerde for allowing me easy access to Tulane's the William Ransom Hogan Jazz Archives. A special thanks also to Professor Frank Tirro of Yale University for the interest that he has shown in my projects over the years and for his many helpful suggestions and comments. To Professor Egydio de Castro e Silva of Tulane I am deeply grateful for having read the entire manuscript and for the encouragement he has offered from the beginning.

Among my colleagues at the University of New Orleans, Professor Paul Sandford of the Department of History contributed many useful insights concerning jazz developments before and after World War II, and the staffs of the Music Listening Room and WWNO-FM provided recordings for my use that otherwise would have been unavailable.

A study such as this would not be possible without the friendly guidance of performing jazz musicians. I therefore send my thanks to Bill Huntington of Loyola University in New Orleans and to Hank Mackie, Charlie Miller, and Dennis Wilson, all of whom read the entire manuscript and contributed many helpful suggestions.

But most of all I would like to thank Sonny Rollins, who so patiently answered all of my questions and whose refreshing attitude about music, and modest assessment of his own contribution, made this entire undertaking worthwhile.

Charles Blancq

University of New Orleans

Chronology

1930 Theodore Walter "Sonny" Rollins born 7 September, in New York City.

1944 Begins study of alto saxophone while still in high school.

1946 Switches from alto to tenor saxophone.

1947 Graduates from Benjamin Franklin High School. Joins musician's union and begins working professionally in New York.

1948—1949 Makes first recordings with Babs Gonzales, Bud Powell, and J. J. Johnson.

1950 First trip to Chicago to work with drummer Ike Day.

1951 Joins the Miles Davis Quintet—remains through the year. Makes first recordings as a leader.

1955 Checks into the Public Service Hospital, Lexington, Kentucky. Moves to Chicago to convalesce. Joins the Max Roach/Clifford Brown Quintet. Remains with this organization until 1957.

1956 Records *Brilliant Corners* with Thelonious Monk, *Tenor Madness* with John Coltrane, and *Saxophone Collossus* under his own name.

1957 First trip to California; records *Way Out West;* meets Ornette Coleman. Leaves Max Roach and forms piano-less trio, group stays together through the summer of 1959.

1958 Records *The Freedom Suite*, his first extended composition.

1959 First European tour.

1959—1961 First retirement (The "bridge" sabbatical).

1961   Ends first sabbatical with an appearance at the Jazz Gallery.

1962   Records *The Bridge* for RCA, first recording since 1959. Records *What's New?* for RCA. Begins free jazz experiments.

1963   Appears at the Newport Jazz Festival with guest Coleman Hawkins. Tours Japan. Records *Sonny Meets Hawk.*

1965   *There Will Never Be Another You,* his first recording for Impulse Records. Scores and records (in London) the sound track for the film *Alfie.*

1968   Journeys to Japan to study Zen and Vedanta.

1969   Second tour of Japan.

1969—1971   Second sabbatical, retires completely from music.

1972   *Sonny Rollins's Next Album,* his first for Milestone Records. Awarded a Guggenheim Fellowship. Moves from Brooklyn to Germantown, N.Y.

1973   Elected as the 38th member of the Downbeat Hall of Fame.

1974   *The Cutting Edge* awarded the "Grand Prix du Disque."

1974—1980   Records eight more albums for Milestone, all produced by Orrin Keepnews.

1979   Guest appearance on NBC's "Tonight show—plays unaccompanied tenor solo.

1981   Appears as guest soloist on the recording *The Rolling Stones: Tattoo You* (Rolling Stone Records, Musidor B.V., COC 16052).

1

Rollins the Musician

The Preprofessional Years

A family in Harlem

Harlem during the 1930s was a formidable location for the breeding of a jazz musician. Its population increased substantially during the years between World War I and World War II, making it the nation's largest black community and the residential and cultural center for Afro-American art of all types. There were restaurants, night clubs, ballrooms and after-hour clubs of every description. Music, particularly, jazz and blues, played an important role in the community's development, entertainment, and cultural life.

Such was the milieu in which Sonny Rollins was born on 7 September, 1930. Named Walter Theodore Rollins (he later reversed the order of his first and middle names to Theodore Walter) he could not have begun life in a more stimulating atmosphere. Raised by his mother, a native of the Virgin Islands and a domestic, who often worked for wealthy white families on Park Avenue, the family moved several times during his youth: from his birthplace on 137th Street, between Lennox and 7th Avenues, to 138th Street and later to 136th Street and 135th Street. When Rollins was nine years old, the family made a fortuitous move to an apartment on 153rd Street in the Sugar Hill district. Sugar Hill was the most exclusive section of Harlem at the time; it was also the preferred residential area of most of the professional people in the black community—including many prominent jazz musicians.

The Rollins family was a musical one. Sonny's older sister played piano and sang in church and his older brother, a violinist, was proficient enough to attract the attention of the Pittsburgh Symphony Orchestra (their attempt to recruit him from high school failed, however, and the prospective violinist studied medicine instead). Both brother and sister attended Music and Art High School—a specialized school "only for the best and most talented of kids"[1]—and both had received a considerable amount of formal instruction and training. Sonny received very little.

His father was a career navy man during the 1930s and 1940s and traveled most of the time. Sonny remembers meeting him for the first time when he was about three years old: "I was afraid of him; here was this great big guy with a deep voice. . . . He was away at sea a lot so I saw little of him, but it wasn't a case of him not being there at all." Some years later, Rollins recalled, he would spend his summer vacations working on the naval base at Annapolis, where his father was in charge of an officers' club. "He had risen to the rank of Chief Petty Officer and that was about as high as a black could go in the Navy at that time." Although not a professional musician, the elder Rollins played the clarinet as a young man and, perhaps because of this, encouraged all of the children to be musical.

Rollins started on the piano when he was eight years old but failed to respond to music lessons "because [they were] forced upon me." By age eleven, his disposition had changed: a glimpse of his uncle's shiny saxophone ("he showed it to me when I was visiting him one day") convinced him to pursue music. Even though times were hard, his mother eventually saved enough to buy him a sax, first an alto and later a tenor.

Musical education

In contrast with the training of performers who play in the "classical" tradition, the education of the jazz musician of the 1930s and 1940s was largely without the aid of written music or formal instruction. The information was transmitted from one generation of players to the next in the master-apprentice fashion and the jazz performer became familiar with the traditions and style of his forbears primarily by hearing live performances, or through the study of phonograph recordings. This method of transmission exists because, throughout the history of jazz, the players have always demonstrated their skills in performance rather than by communicating them verbally or in writing.

The early music education of Sonny Rollins appears to have followed this same pattern. With the exception of some isolated modestly priced private lessons on 48th Street, the location of many music stores and small teaching studios, Rollins is a self-taught performer. Being self-taught does not mean that he lacks formal training altogether, only that the process was a more casual one than learning in the classroom. Rollins, after all, did play in his high-school band and attempted to study music throughout his high-school years. He even attended traditional harmony classes, "but it was a bad experience for me ... because my music teacher in high school was a woman with whom I did not get along at all. She was my harmony teacher, but the way she taught turned me off from doing counterpoint. It was a very strict method of teaching, parallel fifths and so on. So I really consider myself self-taught because most of what I learned, I learned from other musicians; listening to other guys play, or being around other musicians ... listening to records and so on. I think that what I got from my studying and my lessons was just the basic fundamentals."

One of the "other musicians" that Rollins listened to in his formative years was the alto saxophonist Louis Jordan. Jordan's Tympany Five were a successful rhythm and blues group, but had a style close to jazz. Their instrumentation of alto sax, trumpet, and rhythm was the same adopted by the bebop combos of the mid-1940s. "My uncle took care of me a lot, especially when the others were out of the house, and he had recordings of Louis Jordan and a lot of blues records by people like Tommy McClennan, Lonnie Johnson and Arthur 'Big Boy' Crudup. My brother had recordings of Duke Ellington and I listened to them also, but I preferred Louis Jordan ... he played the alto and sang the blues." So the combination of phonograph recordings, a smattering of formal instruction, and a musical family ("my brother was a big influence on me, he practiced his violin all the time and some of that seeped into me when I was very young") played a part in shaping Rollins the young musician. The most significant stimulation, however, came from the neighborhood environment and the rich musical tradition that it provided.

Harlem: A musical environment

Harlem during the late 1930s and early 1940s was the location of numerous jazz clubs and the center of many of the new developments in jazz. Even a casual walk to and from P.S. 89 took Rollins past the legendary Savoy Ballroom and Elk's Rendezvous at West 134th and Lennox Avenue, where a "currently appearing" picture of his idol Louis Jordan was proudly displayed. Furthermore, on Sugar Hill lived many famous jazz musicians such as Don Redman, Erskine Hawkins, Cy Oliver, Andy Kirk, Nat Cole, Denzil Best, and Jimmy Crawford. Rollins met all of them and was awed by their reputations and presence. Coleman Hawkins, recently returned from a five-year stay in Europe, also lived nearby on 153rd Street and had a profound effect on the young Rollins, both personally and musically. "He was different from other musicians," Rollins recalls. "He was playing so much music—so many chord changes and progressions, an intellectualized way of playing. This was musicianship on a very high level . . . this struck me and I liked that about him. I became a Coleman Hawkins fanatic." The often-told story of how Sonny the teenager would wait on Hawkins's doorstep for the older man to return from an engagement is actually true, and Sonny still has the photograph that Coleman autographed for him in 1945.

The pianist Bud Powell was also a neighbor. He lived on the corner of West 141st Street and St. Nicolas Avenue, Rollins and his family on West 153rd and Edgecombe ("for a young kid that was not that far to walk—it was almost the same area"). Powell was closer in age to Rollins than most of the older players and the younger man admired his musicianship. "He seemed to have a lot of training and was always practicing and writing . . . a lot of us used to hang around him, because we looked up to him; he was one of the best players around." Rollins must have absorbed a great deal from these early experiences, for only a few years later (1949) he was to make one of his earliest recordings with his idol (*The Amazing Bud Powell, Vol. I.*).

The Young Professional

Early recordings

Sonny graduated from New York City's Benjamin Franklin High School in 1947. He had played the tenor sax for only two years but already was in the musicians' union and was beginning to work professionally. By 1949 he made his first recording with singer Babs Gonzales, a sometime promoter, disc jockey, and manager who entered into a number of recording ventures with the leading bop musicians of the late 1940s. Others were soon to follow, including the Bud Powell date with Fats Navarro mentioned earlier, and an album (*Mad Bebop*) in 1949 with trombonist J. J. Johnson that included

Sonny's first recorded composition, "Audubon." Things were moving fast now for the nineteen-year-old newcomer: there were many casual engagements, one-nighters, and jam sessions—often in the presence of famous and established performers. After one such jam session at Minton's Playhouse in 1950, Rollins was approached by a local promoter from the audience and invited to appear in a show at the 845 Club in the Bronx the following night. It was to be an All-Star Jam and Rollins's function was to play intermissions between the sets of the big-name performers. As luck would have it, Rollins found himself playing opposite a group fronted by Miles Davis and Bud Powell. His playing apparently impressed Davis enough that the trumpeter offered him a place in his band. "After I came down from playing, Miles came up to me and said, 'Look, man, come on and join my band'... just like that, and that was the beginning of a beautiful friendship."

The Miles Davis Quintet

Sonny's initial stay with the Davis band lasted through 1951, and during that time he recorded several sessions for Prestige Records (later released as *Miles and Horns* [Prestige 7025.], *Dig* [Prestige 7012], and *Conception* [Prestige 7013]). All were Davis's dates, but Rollins's performance on the *Conception* recording led his first contract with Prestige. These were important events for the twenty-one-year-old Rollins, because through these recordings he made his first public impression as a professional jazz musician. All of the trademarks of his more mature style are present: the big tenor sound, especially in the low register, and the easy melodic approach to improvising marked by the unique manner in which he shapes his melodic lines—always avoiding the obvious resolution and sequence. There is also the highly original rhythmic concept: a continuous boplike line with many unhurried embellishments. All in all, he appears more the seasoned veteran than the precocious newcomer that he was.

Rollins would return to play with Miles's band at various times throughout the 1950s, but in the meantime he freelanced, appearing with drummer Ike Day in Chicago during 1951, returning again to Chicago for an appearance at the Beehive in 1954. Because of his East Coast orientation, he devoted much of his time to engagements in the New York area. But there were some idle moments also, and part of the time he didn't work at all.

The bout with drugs

The year after graduating from high school Rollins developed a dependency on drugs. Heroin addiction was not uncommon among jazz musicians of this period. Charlie Parker began his addiction when he was fifteen and it stayed with him the rest of his life. And the legends and the rumors surrounding Parker, his music and life-style both, were impressive enough that many younger musicians followed his example. "He was our hero, our leader . . . a father figure . . . he couldn't come off the bandstand without us crowding around him. We must have really bugged him, but he was always great to us, always tolerant and nice." Rollins recorded with Parker as early as 1948 or 1949 and again in 1953. During the 1953 encounter, a record date with Miles Davis, Sonny told the older man that he was "clean" (from drugs) when he actually wasn't. Parker was delighted: "he was so happy, but when he learned the truth, he was really upset about it . . . Bird didn't want anybody else to be like him." This incident encouraged Rollins to do something about his condition. In 1955, he enrolled in the detoxification program at the United States Public Service Hospital in Lexington, Kentucky. "This was a voluntary program and you could leave any time you wanted to. You weren't under any sentence, but to get the complete cure it took four and a half months." Rollins went the full term and was clinically "cured," but his return to professional music was necessarily slow and cautious. The night-club environment on the East Coast would be a tough one to face at this point in his life, so he decided to brace himself for the challenging return. He moved to Chicago. "After Lexington, I began the long road back . . . I had alienated most of my friends doing the things you do when you're hooked on drugs. I wasn't quite strong enough to be around clubs so I moved to Chicago and worked a series of day jobs."

Rollins's room at the Chicago Y.M.C.A. was small but comfortable, and the job they gave him provided him with a modest income. Here he could convalesce, practicing at night and working and walking during the days, until he felt strong enough to go back to night clubs. He didn't have to wait long. In November 1955, the prestigous Max Roach/Clifford Brown Quintet came to town and their saxophonist, Harold Land, had to leave for California—his wife was having a baby. Rollins was ready to return to full-time playing, and he did.

The Brown/Roach Association

Rollins first met Clifford Brown on a recording date sometime in the early 1950s. He had composed an original tune, "Carvin' the Rocks," and another, "Bella Rosa," in conjunction with pianist Elmo Hope. Both were used in Clifford's session, and the trumpeter was very impressed.

Clifford possessed a demeanor that Rollins particularly admired ("he was so humble and beautiful") and of course his musicianship was quite advanced for his years. The winner of the New Star Award in the 1954 Downbeat Critics Poll "Brownie," as he was known, was one of the brightest young trumpeters of his generation. His tragic death during the summer of 1956 (the group's pianist, Richie Powell, Bud's younger brother, was in the car with him and was also killed) was a devasting loss for the jazz world. It was an especially hard loss for Rollins, who, during this period of rehabilitation was guided by Brown's cheerful disposition and his conviction that an inspired jazzman need not be dependent on drugs. The band also boasted bassist George Morrow, a San Francisco-based freelancer, and the innovative drumming of Max Roach.

The Brown/Roach Quintet was among the top two or three jazz combos of the 1950s, and many feel that some of Rollins's best work was recorded with this group and with Roach's new quintet formed after Brown's and Powell's deaths. Rollins was absolutely in top form during his nineteen months with Roach. His power as a soloist rapidly maturing, he became a regular feature during the band's blistering fast tunes and romantic ballads. His classic performances of "Just One of Those Things," "Woodyn' You," "What Is This Thing Called Love" and "Body and Soul" reveal a twenty-six-year-old melodic improviser who was the equal of any jazz performer of that time.

Sonny made his first trip to California with the quintet in March 1957. The West Coast was fertile jazz territory at that time; there were many jazz clubs, and the Brown/Roach group must have appeared in sharp relief to the then prevalent sound of "cool" jazz. The trip also provided Sonny with the opportunity to do something that he had wanted to do for a long time: record without a pianist, just bass and drums. The piano had traditionally played an harmonic role in even the earliest jazz bands when backing a soloist; but Rollins felt that without the piano, the soloist had more freedom or harmonic space to improvise. The outcome of this experiment can be heard on *Way Out West* (Contemporary C3530). Joined by bassist Ray Brown and drummer Shelly Manne (both winners of the number-one spots in the 1956 *Downbeat*, *Metronome*, and *Playboy* popularity polls), Rollins put together an album of four standards and two originals that still ranks among his very best recordings. The feat is all the more remarkable when one considers that the three had never before played or recorded together and the session had to be called at 3:00 A.M.—the only time that all were free from their regular music engagements.

Goes Independent

Rollins left the Max Roach Quintet in May 1957 and appeared with Miles Davis at the Café Bohemia (replacing John Coltrane) before organizing his own group for an engagement at the Village Vanguard. He was a leader now, and a well respected one at that. The years 1955—1957 were among the most productive of his career: in addition to the activities with Roach, he made recordings and/or appearances with Thelonious Monk (*Brilliant Corners*, Riverside 226), John Coltrane (*Tenor Madness*, Prestige 7047), and some under his own name with a rhythm section borrowed from the Miles Davis Quintet. And then there was *Saxophone Colossus* (recorded in June 1956), the most critically discussed and analyzed recording of his career.

The group he formed for the Village Vanguard appearance included, at first, Donald Byrd on trumpet, along with piano, bass, and drums. After the first week, and many piano tryouts, Rollins eliminated both piano and trumpet and settled on bass and drums only—an instrumentation he was to prefer for the next two years. Rollins was not the first jazzman to play without a piano. The baritone saxophonist Gerry Mulligan had done so in the early 1950s. The change, however, was an indication of an increasing frustration on Rollins's part, a frustration that eventually would culminate in his retiring from public performance altogether. The elimination of the piano from the group and the reach for new freedom in his playing was really Rollins's attempt to sustain the reputation that he so justly earned, but was still not secure. Here, perhaps as a result, began an increasing interest in totally unaccompanied "solo" playing ("It Could Happen to You" was the first example, recorded in June 1957).

Rollins would repeat experiments of this kind and eventually become known for unaccompanied playing—one of the few major non-keyboard jazzmen to attempt such a feat on a consistent basis.

The First Sabbatical

What does a jazzman do when he feels he is losing contact with his audience? When he senses, rightly or wrongly, that his creative powers are gradually ebbing away? He retires; at least that is what Sonny Rollins did. "The reasons for my taking that first sabbatical get back to my being self-taught—my always trying to improve my playing ... I was receiving much publicity in the jazz world, but felt inadequate at certain tasks ... I wanted more training, to study more. I was getting more acclaim than I could handle and a name that I felt I couldn't support." Rollins's motives for retiring, therefore, apparently were entirely musical.

For Rollins, this sabbatical meant a complete withdrawal from the world of active performing—no more engagements of any kind. He would practice, study composition and music theory, and undertake a physical-fitness program. But the small Lower East Side apartment that he shared with his wife, Lucille, was not totally conducive to this new spartan life-style. This was a congested neighborhood, affording little privacy; his constant practicing began to disturb the neighbors, especially a yong pregnant girl nearby, who was about to give birth to her baby. Always resourceful, Rollins found the solution he had been seeking in his own neighborhood: the Williamsburg Bridge.

The bridge

One of three suspension bridges that span the East River and link Manhattan with Brooklyn, the Williamsburg is a large, imposing structure with a pedestrian walkway high above the auto traffic corridor. Here Rollins would undertake his musical and physical fitness program. The long uninterrupted walkway was perfect for jogging, practicing, or just strolling. Parts of the superstructure even served as a kind of makeshift gymnasium, where he could chin himself and perform various other excercises. An occasional athlete would jog by, but otherwise it was an isolated spot and the noise of the traffic below drowned out the sound of his playing—his privacy was thus assured.[2] Privacy, concentration, and excercise were really the main objectives of Rollins's two-year hiatus—but although reclusive, he was not totally removed from the world of music. He took music lessons at the Henry Street School ("a community school—one of the oldest in New York that taught neighborhood people music. It was located right down the street from where I lived and there was an instructor there who was recommended to me by a friend in San Francisco") and he maintained close contact with other musicians during this period.

Ornette Coleman and John Coltrane

The period of Rollins's retirement was an extremely volatile time for jazz, with new styles and personalities rapidly emerging even before the older ones were fully assimilated. Alto saxophonist Ornette Coleman, the leader of the new "free jazz" movement, was appearing at the Five Spot Café and the controversy he sparked seemed to close the ranks of the avant-garde around him. John Coltrane, having left the Miles Davis Quintet, was forming his own groups and he too was moving closer to the free jazz by introducing African and Asian musical strains into his playing. Rollins, actually the youngest of the three (Coltrane was born in 1926 and Coleman a few months before Rollins in 1930), seemed senior by reputation. His precocious start and his personal acquaintance with the leading figures of bebop in Harlem gave him an entrance to jazz circles at age nineteen. Coltrane, on the other hand, was really not well known before he joined Miles Davis in 1955 (he was twenty-nine) and Coleman, an even more obscure and puzzling figure, was also twenty-nine when he made his New York debut.

Rollins had known both of them for some time. He met John Coltrane many years earlier when he (Rollins) first played with Miles Davis; and Ornette, on his first trip to California in 1957 ("We used to go down to the beach and practice at the Pacific Ocean together"). Rollins considered them personal friends. "I was probably closer to John, . . . but both he and Ornette came by my house when I was 'on the bridge' . . . we had a lot of contact during that time."

Rollins also frequented various jazz clubs during his retirement and recalls one evening in particular when he heard Ornette at the Five Spot Café. "I had been to the Jazz Gallery earlier and there was a bebop group playing there. There were no people in the place and the group sounded old-fashioned and played with a conventional rhythmic concept. And then I went to hear Ornette at the Five

Spot. The place was alive and crowded and the music fresh sounding, especially the rhythmic concept, because of Billy Higgins's drumming."

Prepares to come back

Twenty-one months into his self-imposed sabbatical Rollins was achieving nearly all of his objectives: his life was comfortable and productive and centered around a daily routine of practice and excercise—just the way he had planned. With Lucille working as an executive secretary in Manhattan and royalty checks from recordings coming in, there were few monetary concerns. (Contrary to reports that he drove a cab during this period, Rollins took neither musical nor nonmusical work; he was totally unemployed.) But he knew that the longer he put off his return to professional activities, the more difficult that decision would be to make. By the fall of 1961, he was ready to come back and he announced his return for an engagement at New York's Jazz Gallery, the celebrated jazz showroom in downtown Manhattan.

The Return

There was as much publicity about Sonny's return to active playing as there was curiosity about why he had retired in the first place. Why would a performer of Rollins's stature voluntarily withdraw from public appearances at the very height of critical acclaim, and what prompted him to come back after nearly two years? The consensus among many critics, listeners, and, to a lesser extent, musicians was that Sonny had suffered some kind of musical breakdown, that the growing reputations of John Coltrane and younger saxophonists had forced his retirement.[3] But Rollins quickly dispelled those rumors with a series of patient interviews in which he clarified his absence as a voluntary one, undertaken for reasons of self-improvement. Any suspicions that some ill had befallen him were quickly put to rest, anyway, with his performance at the Jazz Gallery. The reviews were almost unanimously enthusiastic. "Sonny Rollins returns as strong or stronger than ever" read one, and the majority of critics were relieved to have him back, perhaps too relieved to notice that Rollins had adopted an entirely new perspective. Jazz itself had changed, of course, and Rollins was preparing to find a place in the new music.

The 1960s: Years of Uncertainty

The acceptance or rejection of Sonny Rollins's foray into the free jazz of the early 1960s depends entirely upon one's perspective of the tenor player's career in music. For those familiar with his progress during the 1950s, his new stance seemed senseless and disappointing, a complete departure from his earlier style with no apparent justification for the change. But Rollins, faced with all the new developments that occurred during his two-year absence, could not continue his melodic style of the 1950s. His longstanding quest for self-improvement compelled him to follow the free jazz lead set by Coleman, Coltrane, and their disciples.

Some critics and listeners welcomed Rollins's entry in the avant-garde. As an established player he could lend the movement the credibility that others could not give it. For Rollins, however, it proved to be one of the most challenging periods of his long career. Jazz itself was in trouble. Even before the Beatles practically revolutionized the popular music industry overnight, audiences were quickly losing interest in "experimental jazz." Many jazz clubs closed during this period—some never to open again. By the time Rollins committed himself to a freer style of playing, the novelty was beginning to wear off. Ornette Coleman, having survived three years of some of the sharpest criticism ever directed at a jazz musician, went into temporary retirement.

Rollins, however, still felt that further development of free, collective improvisation was possible and, within a few months of recording *The Bridge* (RCA LPM 2527), he formed a group composed of two of Ornette Coleman's former sidemen, trumpeter Don Cherry and drummer Billy Higgins.

Rollins, Cherry, Higgins, and a number of bass players continued to play together for all of 1962 and part of 1963. There was a European tour with concerts in Germany and Austria during which Sonny's playing became increasingly abstract. He was playing mixed programs of familiar standards and free jazz originals, but regardless of the type of material, his style of improvising remained the same: uninhibited, free, and nonmelodic.

Less activity and another sabbatical

The 1960s were not the most productive years for Sonny Rollins. There was an occasional concert or solo set, two tours of Japan—the first in 1963 and again in 1968—and various club dates, including one at Ronnie Scott's in London (which led to Rollins's part in scoring and recording the sound track of the film *Alfie* in 1965). But compared to the decade before, when first as a sideman and later as a leader Rollins made over three dozen recordings, he recorded only twelve LPs between the years 1962 and 1969. And they were uneven recordings, made with varying personnel and some surprising changes in material. For a brief time in 1965, for example, he seemed to revert to more standard tunes (*There Will Never Be Another You* [Impulse IA-9349] and *On Impulse* [Impulse A-91]), but even here his improvisatory style was still very free.

Like many jazz musicians of this period who were searching for a deeper meaning in their music and life, Rollins sought to enrich his through a new physical and spiritual awakening. The squalid night-club environment in which he was forced to work did little to satisfy his desire for mental and physical self-improvement—the goals that motivated his first retirement. Only through some uplifting experience could he hope to sustain himself and continue to be a productive jazz musician. The two tours of Japan provided Rollins with the answer and left him with a lifelong interest in Zen. In fact, so moved was he by his second Japanese tour, he returned for a third time to the Orient, this time to India, where he lived in an ashram (a meeting place for religious instruction and excercise). His four months in this monastic setting (January-May 1968) were filled with the study of yoga and Hindu philosophy, along with some exposure to Indian music. This was not a musical sabbatical, but Rollins did play his saxophone on occasion with the local musicians. He also composed songs and, in Bombay, heard concerts by outstanding Indian musicians ("these were usually very long affairs—lasting seven or eight hours").

The move toward pop/jazz

At first Sonny felt good upon his return home; he concertized and renewed his club work. But the uncertainty of the 1960s had taken its toll on virtually all jazz musicians, Rollins included. His physical appearance varied often during these years, as did his deportment on stage. A typical Sonny Rollins set during the 1960s might have begun with the band playing while Rollins emerged from behind the stage or from the audience. He also developed a habit of increased movement while playing, and additional microphones were needed to permit him to do this. (This problem was eventually solved by attaching a microphone to his saxophone.) In short, every concession was made to allow for the maximum amount of freedom in the performance.

Such antics might seem trivial or silly coming from a performer of Rollins's reputation, but his behavior was consistent with a general concern shared by many jazz musicians of this time. Free jazz afforded the players greater freedom in improvising, but it also made increased demands on the ability of the audience to understand the music. There began a "comprehension gap" between musician and audience that pushed the players to the brink of even more daring experiments. If the listener could not participate in the exhilaration of abstract, free improvisation as the player did, then perhaps some other aspect of the performance could be appealing. The net result was an increase in showmanship and an attempt to gain larger (although perhaps less discriminatory) audiences. By the late 1960s, the night club was beginning to be a less favorable setting for hearing jazz than the concert hall or festival. A jazz concert became an "event" and was superficially celebrated in much the same way as that of the rock festival. It was the beginning of a new era, the era of pop/jazz, and Sonny Rollins was one of many name jazz musicians who would welcome the change and explore its potential.

The 1970s: A Jazz Renaissance

The 1970s began with Sonny Rollins on still another sabbatical.[4] The year after his return from India had been a frustrating one for the thirty-nine-year-old performer. Problems with agents, night-club owners, and the night-club business in general compelled him to withdraw from public performance once again. But unlike his other sabbaticals, during which he sought to refresh himself musically, he would retire from music altogether on this one, and not play his horn at all for the next twenty months.

Sonny returned to recording during the summer of 1972 with *Sonny Rollins' Next Album* and a new record company, Milestone—the label that he has remained with to this day. The 1970s would eventually go well for Rollins. Jazz and particuarly pop/jazz found new acceptance among larger audiences, especially younger audiences. By 1972, the jazz/rock fusion had grown beyond anyone's expectations and hardly a major jazz performer could remain unaffected by its success. But Rollins steered away from the more esoteric and progressive experiments of Weather Report, Herbie Hancock, Chick Corea, and Miles Davis, preferring a simpler eclectic mixture of calypso, blues, and contemporary dance tunes instead. He composed a lot during the 1970s and his originals made up a substantial proportion of his recorded output. Simplicity is their main attribute; simplicity of form, melody, and rhythm. His own playing reflects his new attitude in an improvisational style that includes more repetition and less complex melodic lines. Once again, critics, listeners, and musicians alike were confused by his surprisingly independent course. Why such a simple orientation, when mainstream jazz seemed headed toward increasing virtuosity? Only Rollins can answer that question with certainty, of course, but the indications are that after the difficult avant-garde years of the 1960s, he, like many other jazzmen, was ready to resume contact with the estranged jazz audiences.

Sonny, in fact, probably enjoyed more public recognition during the 1970s than at any other time in his career. He received a Guggenheim Fellowship in 1972 (to work on an extended composition for saxophone), was elected as the thirty-eighth member to the Downbeat Hall of Fame in 1973, and in 1979 performed an unaccompanied tenor solo on NBC's "Tonight" show. His guest appearance on this popular talk show is unprecedented for a jazzman of his caliber.

So, as a player of the 1970s, Rollins perhaps found the freedom that he sought for so long. Sabbaticals are no longer necessary now; his status as veteran jazzman and popular performer has enabled him to pick and choose engagements at will. He travels less ("It's grueling for me on the road—I put a lot into it"), and even when he is working he prefers a ratio of perhaps three weeks on and two off. But the journey is not over yet. Sonny Rollins is still the restless searcher in pursuit of an elusive goal.

2

Jazz Improvisation

Traditional Views and Misconceptions

As an improvised art form of Afro-American origins, jazz has always been easily differentiated from other kinds of music. Yet the precise nature and extent of improvisation in the jazz performance has only been partially understood. Frank Tirro, in his article "Constructive Elements in Jazz Improvisation," refers to improvisation as "the somewhat mystical art of performing music as an immediate reproduction of simultaneous mental processes...."[1] The term "mystical" is particularly appropriate when applied to jazz improvisation because of the numerous misconceptions that have always surrounded the music. Jazz has traditionally been viewed as a spontaneous musical creation unique to a certain performance, the exact realization of which could not be duplicated in future performances. This is in contrast to the performance of composed or "fixed" music, as found in the European Art-Music tradition, which has as its aim the precise recreation of a composer's intention, an accurate and faithful rendition of the creator's design.

While concepts like these have served for many years to distinguish these two basic approaches to performing music, they must be regarded as largely theoretical distinctions that encourage an erroneous view of the nature of jazz improvisation. Simply stated, this misconception is that, when improvising, the jazz performer functions without any preconceived plan or order and simply plays anything that "comes into his head." "The fleeting, impermanent nature of improvisational compositions has on occasion led to the faulty notion that the improviser is a sort of musical free agent who is

17

bound by no conventions, and guided by no logic or canon, and who creates music by allowing various and sundry bits of inspiration to 'pop into his mind' and out of his voice or instrument at one and the same time."[2]

Superficial explanations found in even comparatively recent works have overemphasized the role of total spontaneity in jazz performances. The article found in the *Harvard Dictionary of Music*, for example, defines improvisation as "The art of performing music spontaneously, without the aid of manuscript, sketches or memory."[3] This is not completely accurate in describing the improvisations of the great masters, and it is even less true of the highly structured nature of jazz improvisation.

> ...for although memory is not used to recall in detail a once-learned, notated composition for a present-time performance, memory is used to recall the details of the style in which the improviser is performing; and it will be demonstrated that memory recalls, consciously or subconsciously, musical events, patterns, and sound combinations that have become part of the improviser's musical self. Sketches are used—sometimes written and sometimes memorized. Schemata, or models, exist in jazz, and these are the patterns, collections of patterns, or modifications of patterns which form the framework upon which, or against which, the improviser builds his new compositions.[4]

Additional evidence that jazz improvisation is, to some extent at least, premeditated can be seen in the manner in which the jazz performer prepares for his improvised performance. A recorded jazz performance seldom represents the player's first attempt at improvising on a particular tune. Jazz performance can be more accurately seen, in fact, as a continuing process, where, in subsequent performances of the same tune, the player works and reworks material he used before, so that the final recorded version is often a composite of previous performances.[5]

Therefore, while improvisation forms an integral part of a jazz performance, and indeed may be one of the factors distinguishing a jazz performance from a nonjazz performance, it is not the only kind of musical activity found in jazz. A typical jazz performance consists of a mixture of improvised, quasi-improvised, and nonimprovised sections. The fixed or nonimprovised sections are especially evident in the jazz of the 1930s and early 1940s—the so-called "Swing Era"— the period of highly stylized arrangements for big bands, whose instrumentation consists of entire sections of brass, reeds, and rhythm instruments. Here the written arrangement was essential to preserve order within the large ensemble. During this period the soloist improvised primarily over the arranged backgrounds, or occasionally, with rhythm section accompaniment, between the arranged sections of the music. But the need for a preconceived plan or structure is not restricted to this era; it persisted well into modern times and, in fact, is basic to the vast majority of jazz performed even today.

The Forms

The standard tune

The typical jazz performance of the early 1940s was based on standard tunes (i.e., well-established popular songs from such media as musical comedy and film), blues, or, less often, jazz originals. For the purposes of our discussion, a "standard" tune is the thirty-two-measure AABA structure, the majority composed between 1920 and 1960. These were the popular tunes of the day and frequently originated from the most popular Broadway shows or films of this time. Standard tunes and blues formed by far the largest category since they were more familiar to the general public and to the musicians themselves, who learned their melodic and harmonic structures in order to use them as vehicles for their improvisations. By the mid-1940s, the performance of standard tunes was beginning to follow a fairly predictable formula: the melody was first paraphrased by the soloist(s) so as to preserve the tune's melodic identity for the listener; and then a series of improvised choruses followed, based on the tune's chord progression. Some writers describe this practice as the theme and variation format, but in doing so they fail to distinguish between the procedures used in early jazz and the jazz of the late 1930s and after, where the variations were more often based upon the chord sequence rather than the theme.[6] The principal melodic instruments (trumpets, trombones, saxophones, piano, and guitar) were the usual participants in the melodically improvised portions; the bass and drums were chiefly responsible for keeping a steady pulse and, with the piano and/or guitar, provided the harmonic and rhythmic framework upon which the wind instruments improvised. Beginning with post-World War II jazz, it became common for the bass and drums to solo as well, often rivaling the other instruments in their melodic and rhythmic inventiveness.

At the conclusion of the improvised "choruses," the original theme or melody was usually repeated, occasionally followed by a codalike section called a "tag." The repetition was often exact and occurs almost without exception in post-World War II jazz.[7]

Bebop and the standard tune

The relationship of the jazz tune to the preexisting standard (herein called the "model") is obvious when the performer merely embellishes the original (e.g., Miles Davis paraphrasing George Gershwin's "Summertime"), less obvious when the original melody is never stated directly (e.g., Charlie Parker's version of Gershwin's "Embraceable You"). Another common practice widely used during the bebop period (1940s and early 1950s) was to replace the melody of the model with a new melody or theme based upon the harmonic progression of the original.[8] This new method of constructing a jazz tune allowed the performers considerable freedom to create complex original melodies. In performing these melodies, and improvising on their accompanying harmonic patterns, the bebop musician satisfied an ever-increasing urge for demonstrations of virtuosity and technical bravura, the likes of which and never before occurred in the history of jazz. Because they were derived from standard tunes, well known to jazz players, bebop "originals" in one sense provided a ready-assembled repertoire for jazz improvisation; but their complex melodies, expanded chord progressions, and extreme tempos rendered them performable by only the more technically able players. This may account for the popular view of bebop as an esoteric jazz type and its failure to gain a wide listening and performing public. To conceal further the origins of the new tunes, the titles of the standards were dropped, and in their place appeared new and often whimsical titles such as "Hot House" based on Cole Porter's "What Is This Thing Called Love," "Ko-Ko" based on Ray Noble's "Cherokee," or "Ornithology" based on "How High the Moon," a Nancy Hamilton and Morgan Lewis composition.

Many bebop melodies were first conceived as improvisations and then transcribed as new compositions.[9] Thus the themes and their accompanying harmonic changes were frequently so complex in nature that any resemblance to the original model was completely obscured. Since only the harmonic framework of the model was retained in the transformation, the bebop player/composer escaped the enforcement of copyright laws which protect solely the melodic integrity of a composition.

This change of repertoire, coupled with those changes affecting the harmonic and rhythmic structure of jazz during this period, constitutes the major innovation of bebop and signals the beginning of the modern jazz era. Tunes constructed in this manner provided the challenge that the younger, more experimental players were seeking, and at the same time presented a technical obstacle to the preceding generation of jazz performers from the Swing Era, thereby making it difficult for them to participate in the new music.

Achieving formal coherence in the solo

Spontaneity and predetermined planning, then, play equally important roles in jazz improvisation, and the successful performer balances these two disparate elements during the course of his improvisation. This constitutes the basic challenge to every jazz improviser: to create a rhythmically interesting and melodically cohesive improvised line during the performance, while presenting ideas in a naturally unfolding sequence. To accomplish this, the player must adjust his melodic line to conform with the underlying harmonic structure of the model. Ideally, the experienced player does not ramble, quote incoherently, or otherwise "fill up time" with redundant or unrelated material. The idea of avoiding redundancy is central to understanding jazz and how it differs from other forms of more popular music. The simplicity of a tune's structure, its uniformity and repetition, are the essential ingredients of "pop" music, allowing the listener to become quickly familiar with a certain melody or theme. This familiarity is important, because the tune must be easily recalled if it is to be popular. The perceptive enjoyment of a jazz performance, on the other hand, is based on the assumption that the listener is already familiar with the standard jazz repertory, that the player may freely use paraphrase, elision, and irregular phrasing, and that the listener is capable of following the forward progress of the tune and "filling in" the missing parts. The practice of ridding a performance of the redundant elements and of avoiding the obvious is a premise basic to the understanding of all contemporary jazz, and is chiefly responsible for lending jazz a sophistication not found in less esoteric forms of popular music.[10]

Not surprisingly, only a relatively small number of jazz performers have succeeded at the level of performance described above, and among them the great melodic improvisers of all time: Louis Armstrong, Coleman Hawkins, Lester Young, Charlie Parker, Clifford Brown, and Miles Davis. Some of the recordings made by tenor saxophonist Sonny Rollins, place him among this select group, and he may be, as jazz writer Gunther Schuller believes, the first jazz performer to solve the problem of continuity in the improvised line by means of "thematic" improvisation.[11] Thematic improvisation in this context refers to the practice of extemporizing on the theme, or parts thereof, and differs from earlier jazz practices in that the theme is not merely paraphrased but is treated in a developmental way. Earlier approaches to improvisation were largely episodic in nature. Although the improvised line coincided with the harmonic changes sounding at the moment, there was little relationship between one section of the improvised solo and another, so that the overall structure consisted, for the most part, of a juxtaposition of contrasting melodic ideas.

Before investigating the details of Rollins's music, it will be necessary to survey the development of melodic improvisation during the 1920s, 1930s, and 1940s. This was a period of great expansion in jazz, a time in which it grew from a relatively simple means of expression with great popular appeal to a medium of great complexity, resulting in substantial changes in its melodic, rhythmic, and harmonic structure. Because of the large numbers of performers involved in this transition and the limited space available, I will illustrate my discussion with examples drawn primarily from four of the principal improvisers of this era: Louis Armstrong, Coleman Hawkins, Dizzy Gillespie, and Charlie Parker.

3

Melodic Improvisation
before Rollins

The melodic aspect of jazz improvisation has been one of the most elusive and perhaps misunderstood components of the music. For many years some doubted that jazz contained melody at all. Questions such as "Where's the Melody?" and "Who's playing the theme?" were not uncommon reactions from uninformed audiences after hearing a jazz rendition of a familiar tune. To some extent, at least, these concerns were understandable. The rhythmic vitality of much early jazz relegated its melody to a secondary role. After all, jazz was distinguishable from other kinds of music primarily because of its peculiar rhythmic momentum, particularly the element known as "swing."[1] Only with the abandonment of the collective improvisation format of the 1920s and the emergence of the jazz soloist as the principal front-line performer did the melodic ingredient of jazz become more fully recognized. Since that time, the melodic improviser has been a constant presence in most jazz, although his role has varied greatly during the sixty-year history of recorded jazz performances.

King Oliver and Louis Armstrong

The earliest recorded jazz contained little solo improvisation, and the quasi-improvised portions performed "collectively" were sometimes not improvised at all, as subsequent recordings of the same tune show. Comparisons, for example, of recordings by the Original Dixieland Jazz Band made in England in 1919 with recordings of the same tunes made earlier reveal that the "improvised" choruses were, in fact, the same. They had been memorized by the players, and perhaps even rehearsed. Their intention was to give the impression to the audience that the band was improvising, and frequent claims were made by the members of their inability to read music, as if to reinforce this point.[2] The melody was often difficult to discern in early jazz recordings, for it was frequently obscured by a cluttered musical texture, resulting from the "front line" instruments (trumpet or cornet, clarinet, and trombone) attempting to ornament the melody collectively. Collective improvisation lacked the clarity of solo improvisation and was only improvisation in the limited sense anyway, since the melody was closely followed and no single player was charged with maintaining a solo for a prolonged period of time. The most common technique was that of melodic variation, a procedure that resulted in a series of variations on the tune's theme. Unlike the jazz of the 1930s and 1940s, the theme served as a point of departure for the improviser and therefore played an important role in early jazz. Lacking the skill for chordal improvisation (i.e., that based on a chordal sequence), many early players often organized their improvisations by embellishing the theme. The most representative early group employing this technique was that led by the New Orleans-born cornetist Joe "King" Oliver.

The Creole Jazz Band, as it was named by Oliver, was the most disciplined performing group of its day, and contained among its members the first great jazz soloist, Louis Armstrong. Armstrong was engaged by Oliver in 1922 to play second cornet to the leader, and this he did with such authority and aplomb that on many occasions he overshadowed Oliver himself. The emphasis still was on collective improvisation, however, for the 1923 recordings demonstrate that neither Oliver nor Armstrong was capable of consistently producing a fully developed solo. Oliver's contributions rest primarily in his easy, subtle sense of rhythmic swing and his skillful paraphrasing of the theme, and Armstrong's in his clever manipulation of the supporting harmonies to form counterthemes, complementing those of Oliver. The little solo playing that did take place was restricted to occasional choruses and "breaks" (i.e., brief two-measure segments connecting the end of one chorus and the beginning of another, or short solo "fills" that occur in the middle of choruses). In many respects these breaks were the most progressive segments of the performances, since they gradually led to attempts at more extended solos. Armstrong's function within the Oliver organization was strictly secondary to Oliver himself; therefore, whatever abilities he possessed as a soloist were not completely realized until he joined the Fletcher Henderson Orchestra in 1924.

Even the earliest recordings made with the Henderson band clearly show Armstrong to be the outstanding soloist within the group, no small accomplishment since the personnel included some of the finest players of the day, such as trombonist Charlie Green and the Memphis clarinetist Buster Bailey, as well as saxophonist Coleman Hawkins. It was the recordings with Henderson and those that followed with his own Hot Five and Hot Seven groups in Chicago that established Armstrong as the first jazz performer capable of sustaining a coherent improvised solo for an extended period of time.

Armstrong's musical achievement was the result of several factors, not the least of which was the remarkably direct way he paraphrased melodies. This entailed an extremely economical choice of notes, so that much of the extraneous melodic material was eliminated. Armstrong, as an improviser, also introduced several technical innovations that were to become closely identified with his style. His liberal use of chromatic and diatonic passing notes imparted both a sense of variety and a lyrical contour to the melodic line. His use of descending arpeggios, ending on an important "changing note" and then rising a large interval (often a melodic seventh), helped to underline important harmonic changes taking place in the tune.[3] Coupled with a relaxed sense of swing and an impeccable sense of timing, Armstrong's recorded performances became the models for later performers well into the 1940s.

Armstrong solved the problem of continuity in his improvisations by adhering closely to the theme. All during his stay with King Oliver and Fletcher Henderson, his principal method was one of ornamented paraphrase of the original melody. In this sense, his improvisations were the result of a true developmental-variation technique. Since phrases of the original theme followed each other in logical fashion, Armstrong's embellished paraphrased choruses did likewise, and therefore in his best recordings each successive chorus appeared to be an outgrowth of the one before. It was not until after 1925 that Armstrong began to abandon the thematic improvisation concept and to construct his solos on the underlying chord pattern; but even here he frequently reverts to the older, more familiar technique of ornamenting the theme or of abandoning both theme and chord changes and constructing the solo according to rhythmic motives, as the 1928 recording of "Muggles" illustrates. Armstrong's use of small rhythmic motives in this recording represents a significant step forward for the improviser, for it became one of the progressive techniques used by improvisers of the 1940s and 1950s.

Chordal Improvisation

The changes taking place in the late 1920s and early 1930s reflect a trend away from the theme-paraphrase technique and toward one based on the harmonic structure of the model. Although a slow and sporadic process, with many older players continuing to use more traditional methods, by the late 1930s the concept of using chord changes as a basis for melodic improvisation was clearly established. The performer best known for his early employment of this technique was tenor saxophonist Coleman Hawkins.

Hawkins was more than an innovative performer; he was also a pioneer in establishing the saxophone as a serious jazz instrument, which for many years previously had functioned largely as a novelty instrument in military bands and vaudeville shows. In addition, he became one of the very first jazzmen to attract international attention. His extended stay in Europe between 1934 and 1939, where he concertized and recorded in Holland, France, Switzerland, England, and Belgium, did much to advance the understanding of American jazz on an international level. But it was the recordings made upon his return to the United States in 1939 and after that enhanced his reputation as a leading jazz improviser. "Body and Soul," for example, recorded in October 1939, clearly illustrates Hawkins's newly perfected style of melodic improvisation—less reliance on the theme and its component motives in favor of the chord structure as the basis for the improvisation. After the first eight measures there is scarcely any reference to the original theme at all. Instead, Hawkins articulates many of the chords in arpeggiated fashion, so that much of the melodic material resembles a series of consecutive arpeggios. In addition to adjusting his improvised line to the existing chords (i.e., those in the original publication), he interpolates additional chords of his own between those of the original, thereby quickening the harmonic rhythm and expanding the harmonic framework from which he can improvise. This practice of introducing "passing chords" to the existing harmonic framework was not new with Hawkins, but did not become a common practice among jazzmen until the middle 1940s.

Hawkins's treatment of the harmony was generally conservative by today's standards. Although he articulated the chord changes with great ease and dexterity (this practice was later known as "running the changes"), his melodic lines contain relatively few passing notes and auxiliary tones, and the arpeggios often occur directly on the strong beats of the measure or beat in symmetrical, unsyncopated rhythmic patterns.

The recordings of the early 1940s, however, show a decreasing dependency on vertical (chordal) improvisation and a growing tendency toward a more purely melodic style. "The Man I Love," recorded in December 1943, contains moments of sheer linear (i.e., nonarpeggiated) improvisation, foreshadowing the style of the late 1940s. The change from the chordal to the linear style is marked by fewer outright arpeggios and the introduction of more scalewise and chromatic movement in the melodies.

In spite of all Hawkins's progressive melodic ideas, however, he remained rhythmically conservative during his entire career. Even the performances recorded in the early 1960s are reminiscent of the rhythmic style of the 1930s in their accentuation. In the earlier recordings, subdivisions of beats fall regularly into groups of two's and four's (eighth notes and sixteenth notes), or, after 1930, occasional groupings of six $\overset{6}{\text{♫♫}}$; rarely is there an uneven grouping of notes, and the regular alternation of accented downbeat and light upbeat occurs with an increasing regularity that detracts from the inventiveness of Hawkins's playing. This was the rhythmic tradition in jazz that Hawkins inherited, and he accepted it without question and retained it virtually intact throughout his career.

Hawkins's effectiveness as an improviser was sometimes restricted by the type of tune upon which he chose to improvise. In the early years of jazz improvisation, the tunes were often rather dull standards with very few chord changes and therefore of static harmonic movement. Tunes such as "The Sheik of Araby" and "My Blue Heaven," while the most popular tunes of the day, had slow and repetitive harmonic schemes and did not supply the harmonic base conducive to imaginative jazz improvisation. Hawkins overcame this difficulty to some extent by the use of the "passing chords" described earlier, but his improvisations still lacked the energy of younger players such as Eddie "Lockjaw" Davis, Dexter Gordon, Ben Webster, or certainly Charlie Parker.[4] Still, he was one of the few older established players to embrace the new bebop style of the mid-1940s, and Rollins himself listed Hawkins as one of his most important early influences.

The Bop Era

By the early 1940s, styles of improvisation based on both the arpeggiation of chords and the use of scale patterns were well established. The theme-paraphrase technique, employed by the early players (Oliver, Armstrong, and others), had long been abandoned by the younger, more progressive musicians and survived primarily in revivals of earlier traditional jazz. This was a period of considerable experimentation in the harmonic, rhythmic, and melodic structure of the music, and the solutions offered by performers such as Dizzy Gillespie, Charlie Parker, and Thelonious Monk constituted some of the most dramatic and sudden new developments ever encountered in the history of jazz.

Chord extension

An important area of change took place in the music's harmonic structure. For some years popular standards used in jazz improvisation had been harmonized primarily with the standard triads, added sixths, and seventh chords. Isolated examples of more complex structures can be found among the more progressive improvisations of saxophonist Lester Young (mid-1930s) and in some "jazz compositions" such as George Gershwin's opera *Porgy and Bess* (1935), but the harmonic language of the majority of jazz performers remained relatively conservative. By the late 1930s, however, it became increasingly common for performers to extend chords by adding ninths, elevenths, and thirteenths as well as their chromatic alterations: the flatted ninth, augmented ninth, and the augmented eleventh and flatted thirteenth. The presence of extended harmonies, however, was initially confined to the accompaniment or to the orchestration (as with Gershwin) and the improvising jazz performer did not make frequent use of these upper partials until the mid-1940s. Alto saxophonist Charlie Parker was among the first to explain his use of these notes in his melodic lines: ". . . It was December 1939. Now I'd been getting bored with the stereotyped changes that were being

used all the time at the time, I kept thinking there's bound to be
something else. Could hear it but couldn't play it.—Well that night I
was working over 'Cherokee' and found that by using the higher
intervals of a chord as the melodic line and backing them with
appropriate changes, I could play the thing I was hearing. I came
alive."[5]

The use of extended chords and their chromatic alterations
dramatically increased the number of notes from which the improvising performer could choose. Instead of being limited to stressing
the four or five tones present in the seventh and ninth chords,
melodic lines could now be formed from as many as ten to twelve
tones, i.e., virtually every note within the chromatic scale. A
dominant-seventh chord, for example, when augmented by the
diatonic and chromatic versions of the ninth, eleventh, and thirteenth, expands from a chord of four tones to a sonority of eleven
tones (see example 1).

Example 1.

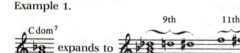

Expansion of the harmonic vocabulary resulted in a corresponding change in the overall contour of the melodic line. Because of the
more liberal use of passing tones, auxiliary tones, and appoggiaturas,
the melodic line now took on a more linear and chromatic appearance (see example 2).

Example 2. Dizzy Gillespie, "52nd Street," meas. 8—11

The majority of jazz performers of the late 1940s were not
"schooled," having had no formal training in the theory of European
art music. While they used a variety of non-harmonic tones intui-

tively and quite liberally, they did not always follow the traditional
resolution patterns. Some nonharmonic tones resolved by skip instead of step, and some, particularly passing-tones, were often not
resolved at all[6] (see example 3).

Example 3. Dizzie Gillespie, "Dizzy Atmosphere," meas. 67—68

In measure 2 of the above example, the normal resolution would
have been to F-natural; but here the dissonant note (E-natural) is
sustained and the resolution is left to the listener's imagination. The
dissonant interval used most often in this manner is the augmented
fourth or flatted fifth, possibly the most characterisic interval of
bebop music.

Other techniques employing melodic dissonance during this
period were even more striking. One common practice was the
superimposition of chords that were not being played in the harmonic accompaniment. Usually this involved outlining a chord
one-half step above (rarely below) the chord prescribed (see example
4).

Example 4. Coleman Hawkins, "Say It Isn't So," meas. 16

On beat four of this example, notes suggesting a Gb chord are
sounded against the F-dominant-seventh chord. Because much of
bebop was performed at extremely fast tempos, dissonant combinations such as these were so quickly resolved that harmonic conflict
was minimized. The same example played at a very slow tempo
would sound considerably more dissonant.

Rhythmic changes

The rhythmic innovations of bebop were almost as startling. From
the very start, jazz rhythm had a strong downbeat orientation, the
tendency to emphasize the metrically strong parts of a measure or
beat. In classic New Orleans jazz equally heavy emphasis was given to

all four beats of the measure; Chicago jazz (of the 1920s) shifted to brighter tempos and alla breve (cut-time) meter emphasizing beats one and three. With the advent of bebop, however, rhythmic stress in the measure changed from the downbeat to the upbeat, so that rhythmic patterns previously accented as ♫♫♩ , for example, are now played ♫♫♩ .

The patterns of accents became so stereotyped in post-World War II jazz and so familiar to the players and educated listeners that it became necessary in practice merely to imply the nonsyncopated notes in the melodic line by attacking them with even less emphasis. This practice, known as "ghosting," is indicated in some of the later musical examples by the use of parentheses, and indicates that the note enclosed is merely suggested rather than sounded emphatically.

Equally important as a rhythmic concept is the soloist's practice of deliberately falling behind the rhythm section's beat. Known as "lagging behind" or "laying back," the sensation of getting behind the beat and then catching up again introduces considerable variety as well as rhythmic tension in the music and seems to be particularly evident in bop and postbop jazz.

Another improvisational mannerism affecting the tempo is the practice of "doubling" the tempo (i.e., playing as if there are twice as many beats per measure) while the rhythm section and therefore the speed of the accompaniment continues in the original tempo. Instances of "double-time" improvisation occur occasionally even in early jazz but are more frequent in the virtuoso performances of the 1940s and after. Again the purpose was to provide rhythmic variety and to generate rhythmic momentum in the solo line.

Finally, the fundamental rhythmic pulse of post-World War II jazz differs substantially from that of earlier periods. The basic beat is not marked nearly as emphatically as it was before, and the regularly recurring accents of early jazz are absent, causing the rhythmic feeling to take on a more subtle sense of swing. Tempos reached much greater extremes, and unlike earlier jazz, where the performers lacked the necessary technical facility to execute very fast tempos, the tempos of bebop often reached speeds of ♩ = 250 and faster. This music was nonfunctional in that it was the first style of jazz that was not specifically intended for dancing. As a result, it tended to be more variable in its tempos and less predictable in its rhythmic accentuation.

Charlie Parker, the consummate performer

The performer generally credited with leading the technical developments in jazz in the mid-1940s is alto saxophonist Charlie
Parker. Parker gets the credit, but a more realistic assessment of his
contribution reveals that he was a relatively passive participant in the
theoretical innovations of the bebop movement. Performers such as
Dizzy Gillespie, Thelonious Monk, Charlie Christian, and Kenny
Clarke were more in the vanguard of the harmonic and technical
developments. Parker seems to have functioned as the supreme
soloist who, more successfully than anyone else, put their ideas into
practice.

Parker's professional recording career spans only fourteen years
(from April 1941, as a sideman with the Jay McShann Orchestra, to
December 1954, his last recording, *Charlie Parker Plays Cole Porter*
[Columbia 33CX10090/Verve 8007]), but his influence has been more
far reaching than possibly any other performer in recent jazz history.
This is due primarily to his highly developed sense of melodic construction and his startling technical virtuosity, far surpassing that of
any other jazz performer of his time or before.

Parker's improvisatory style has been the subject of many studies,
the most recent and thorough being that of Thomas Owens, who
analyzed the motivic construction of Parker's solos.[7] Such a study is
particularly revealing since Parker's approach to melodic improvisation was essentially a motivic one. Owens's transcriptions show that
his solos are based on a repertoire of about one hundred brief
motives which he combined, repeated, and altered in a variety of
ways. Although earlier performers (Hawkins, Lester Young, and
others) had favorite phrases or motives that recur in their playing,
Parker's melodic construction is more consistently dependent on
motives and their episodic repetition.

Motivic construction represents a notable advance in the art of
jazz improvisation, but in Parker's music it sometimes results in a
melodic line of many separate and only remotely related melodic
fragments. This is because the motives did not become the basis of
extended development as they did in European Art music but were
merely "recalled" from time to time as a particular harmonic situa-
tion occurred or as inspiration dictated. Phrases, therefore, sometimes have no direct melodic connection from one to another or to
the theme of the piece. In this sense Parker departs significantly from

the approaches used by Louis Armstrong and later by Miles Davis, both of whom treated improvisation as a more continual process of melodic variation.

So while providing much rhythmic and harmonic excitement for the listener, the melodic continuity of bebop was often difficult to comprehend and by the mid-1950s, having run its course with jazz audiences, it was supplanted by a less extreme and seemingly more appealing style of jazz that began on the East Coast but flourished primarily in California.

The "Cool" Style

"Cool" and "hot" are terms frequently used to describe two opposing trends in jazz performance. The "cool" manner of playing implies understatement, restraint, a striving toward a certain musical purity of expression. The "hot" style, the manner in which most jazz was performed until at least 1935 and intermittently thereafter, refers to an extroverted style, one embracing a very high level of excitement and occasional virtuosity. The West Coast or "cool" style, as it was called, resulted in some significant changes in the basic concept of jazz improvisation. Most important of these was a shift in emphasis from the extroverted "hot" style as exhibited by Gillespie, Parker, and others of the East Coast to a more reserved and introspective style. This was accomplished largely by a change in the overall sound of the music. Unlike the jazz performers of a generation before, the young players of the 1950s were eager to achieve a less abrasive and therefore more appealing sound. The harsh, strident timbre of bebop was abandoned in favor of a more euphonious sound, achieved by a reduction of the volume and the introduction of symphonic instruments into the ensemble. By the early 1950s, the bassoon, tuba, flute, cello, and French horn were familiar instruments in jazz ensembles, and their inclusion resulted in a more orchestral sound, resembling that of a small wind ensemble with jazz-rhythm backgrounds. To exploit this new instrumentation, attention was shifted from the continuous "solo" procedure of bebop to a renewed emphasis on the "arranged" ensemble. The jazz "arrangement," it will be remembered, had not figured prominently in jazz performances since the 1930s and early 1940s, but it was developed with such emphasis during the 1950s that it outweighed in importance the solo portions, thereby weakening the role of improvisation in the performance.

Paradoxically, the individual most responsible for this new direction in jazz had little to do with its subsequent development on the West Coast. Trumpeter Miles Davis and a nine-piece group made what are now regarded as the prototype cool jazz recordings as early as January of 1949. The recordings, later released in 1954 as *The Birth of the Cool* (now available on Capitol DT 1974), were actually the result of three separate recording sessions held during January and April of 1949, and March of 1950. The initial impact upon the public was slight, but they were not ignored by the jazz performers of that time. Davis soon abandoned this large group format but always remained in the vanguard of jazz developments, and emerged as an important improviser after Charlie Parker's death. Reacting against the extreme virtuosity of the bebop school, by the mid-1950s Davis developed a smoothly lyrical style, founded upon theme paraphrase and thematic variation. He used the theme rather than chords as the primary basis for his improvisations and employed fewer notes while often confining his melodic range to the middle and lower registers of the trumpet. The end result was a remarkably lyrical, but spare, melodic style that conformed to the "cool" concept of sonority.

The recordings made by Davis's quintets and those done in collaboration with arranger-composer Gil Evans in the late 1950s are models of the "thematic variation" approach to jazz improvisation. The variation of the theme, it will be remembered, had been the first method used in improvising jazz (employed by Armstrong, Bix Beiderbecke, and others), but was abandoned during the 1930s in favor of the freer, more chordal technique. Davis, then, was reverting to the older approach as a means of achieving cohesion in his solos. His classic performance of Gershwin's "Summertime" (Columbia, CS 8085) illustrates the manner in which he accomplishes this end. This 1958 recording consists of one paraphrased statement, followed by four melodic variations on Gershwin's sixteen-measure theme. The first statement closely adheres to the original theme, but each following variation progresses further from the original. By the third statement, a new motive has been established, based on the raised sixth (G-natural) of the Bb minor scale, and this note figures prominently in both this and the following chorus.

This is true melodic variation in its purest form, for the basis of the improvised performance is the theme itself. Although broken-chord figures are used on the change to Bb major (the thirteenth measure of each chorus), arpeggiation of the harmonic change is generally avoided in favor of a concisely constructed melodic statement interspersed with frequent rests.

In this and other recordings made by Davis about this time, the principal melodic resource was the scale rather than the chord. "I think a movement in jazz is beginning away from the conventional string of chords, and a return to emphasis on melodic rather than harmonic variation. There will be fewer chords but infinite possibilities as to what to do with them."[8] Davis's remarks indicate that his turning to scales as a resource was not accidental, for he was keenly aware of the disjointed effect produced by basing improvisation on chords and the need to seek alternative methods. The new trend was toward scales and modes (other scales produced by starting at different points in the major or minor scale), for he felt that they gave the performer more freedom to create lyrical, uncluttered lines and to produce longer, more cohesive solos.

Thus by the late 1950s, the progressive techniques of jazz improvisation had undergone several distinct transformations: from the simple paraphrase approach, represented primarily in the early jazz of the 1920s and early 1930s (New Orleans and Chicago Dixieland); to a more chordal style that began in the 1930s and continued into the 1940s (Swing); to the chordal-chromatic style based on the extended harmonies of the late 1940s (bebop); to a return once again to improvisation based on the theme. To these may be added still other categories formed by various combinations of these methods. Even as early as the late 1940s, the simultaneous use of two or more techniques was already the norm, even within the confines of a single jazz performance.

As the methods of improvising jazz became more varied, so did the melodic styles. The theme paraphrase-variation technique, as employed by Miles Davis, gave rise to more horizontally conceived melodic lines, those based on scales as the primary structural component. The chordal approach, because of its vertical conception, tended to emphasize the harmonic structure of a tune at the expense of achieving melodic continuity.

By the time of Charlie Parker's death in 1955, jazz improvisation had become so diffuse and varied that no single method or performer appeared strong enough to guarantee its continued development. Parker was considered to be the greatest improviser of all time, for he had seemingly exhausted all the current improvisational resources. If improvisation was to continue progressing, therefore, some new approach was needed, one that would continue to expand the melodic aspect while achieving a coherent musical statement. In 1956, the performer who perfected the next practical solution to the problems of melodic improvisation was tenor saxophonist Theodore "Sonny" Rollins.

Rollins's style of playing through the 1950s is marked by his continuing refinement of the art of melodic improvisation, reaching a peak in the late 1950s and recurring intermittently thereafter. Because his style of playing of the early 1960s shows a noticeable change in direction and approach, it seems appropriate to divide his career into two broad chronological divisions: the first ending with his return from the first sabbatical and the production of the album *The Bridge* (1962); and the second encompassing his forays into the avant-garde, the jazz-rock fusion of the 1960s and the dance trends of the 1970s.

4

The Early Years:
Melody and Rhythm

—

Melody

Jazz melody does not differ substantially from the melody of any other kind of music, except for its occasional fragmentary or "unfinished" quality, a natural consequence of the improvisation process. The spontaneous manner in which most jazz melody is created provides little opportunity for revision or reworking, refinements that are taken for granted in the composition of European art music. The skilled melodic improviser, nevertheless, intuitively strives to fulfill all the laws of tension and relaxation, diversity and balance, and formal proportion found in all good melodies.

Range and shape

Rollins's melodies are of a fairly broad range with an unusually heavy emphasis on the middle to low registers, a facet of his playing perhaps derived from Coleman Hawkins, who was known for his large, powerful sound, particularly in the low register. The shapes of his melodies are vocal in conception and represent a compendium of virtually every approach to melodic style from the conventional practice of reversing direction after large leaps to scalewise passages using various altered and chromatic scales and to occasional jarring, angular lines that twist and turn and seem to defy all the traditional rules of melodic construction. The melodic elements of Rollins's style are extremely heterogeneous and yet the end result is more often than not an extremely balanced and tightly constructed melodic line.

Rollins uses arpeggiation frequently in his melodic construction although such chordal outlines are not used nearly as systematically or as extensively as they were in the music of Coleman Hawkins and his generation. Rollins was primarily concerned with creating melody, and every device used was a means to achieving that end. In addition to varying the contour of the melodic line, he introduced considerable variety in the intensity of the musical expression, from simple, almost songlike lyrical phrases to extremely complex, vertically conceived lines that intricately weave in and out of fast-moving harmonic changes. These two widely divergent melodic approaches along with occasional quotations of unrelated material often appear in an incongruous juxtaposition, an incongruity attributed by some listeners to Rollins's peculiar sense of humor in his playing.

The use of paraphrase

This whimsical, irreverent approach to improvisation is an important part of his technique and is especially evident when he paraphrases a well-known melody. In the jazz of the 1950s, opportunities for paraphrasing the theme came primarily at the beginning of the tune and at the end, where the theme was repeated. A tune's theme was paraphrased because it was being recalled by memory and an exact rendition of the original was considered unnecessary. But Rollins takes the traditional practice of paraphrase a step farther. He often rephrases a familiar melody, stripping it of all its superfluous or redundant components, playing just enough of the original outline to make it recognizable. This is not an uncommon practice among modern jazzmen, but it was developed to a sophisticated degree by Rollins, particularly in the performance of tunes that he played frequently, or ones that are likely to be overly familiar to the listener. The understanding among jazzmen seemed to be that the more familiar a theme was, the less need there was to state it in its totality, and the greater the opportunity for paraphrase. A successful paraphrase, therefore, depends on the listener's familiarity with the tune, for in order for the listener to "fill in" the missing parts, he must be well acquainted with the original version. So skilled is Rollins as a paraphraser, that at least one writer has concluded that he could be regarded a major jazz performer based on his paraphrasing ability alone: "... even if Rollins decided to hereafter play only straight melody, he would still be a creative jazz musician. Because by the time a melody has undergone his singular treatment of singing tone and orgasmic [*sic*] rhythm, it is infused with a vitality that renders it a new thing."[1]

The occasional humor in Rollins's improvised choruses is paralleled by his choice of tunes as models. At a time when most jazz players were trying to free themselves from dependency on simple pop-tune models, Rollins deliberately sought tunes whose melodies had seemingly little to offer as material for jazz improvisation, but whose easy familiarity made his paraphrases all the more striking. There seems, in fact, to have been no limit to the broad range of tune types recorded by Rollins. They included every conceivable kind of material from cowboy songs (*Way Out West,* Contemporary 3530) to vaudeville tunes. This explains his recordings of Noel Coward's "Someday I'll Find You," Sammie Kahn's "Toot Toot Tootsie" (Rollins expressed a particular liking for songs sung by Al Jolson), Clifford Grey's "If You Were the Only Girl in the World," and Irving Berlin's "There's No Business Like Show Business." Hardly typical of the material used by the majority of the jazz players during the late 1950s, Rollins saw in them an opportunity for satire that apparently suited his temperament at that time.

Ornamentation

Rollins amplifies his seemingly casual manner of melodic construction by means of certain melodic embellishments. Melodic ornaments have been standard fare with jazz performers almost from the very beginning of jazz, but in Rollins's music they take on a unique structural importance. His favorite is the gruppetto figure 🎵 identified by some jazz writers as the "jazz turn," because of its frequent use by jazz players. Almost all moderate-tempo performances of Rollins contain some use of this ornament, but in the 1957 recording of "Little Folks" (Mercury MG-36108), the jazz turn becomes the principal organizing motive. Initially on the first beat of measure five, Rollins develops it sequentially on the first beat of each of the next twelve measures with the exception of measure thirteen.

Rollins's melodic style does not appear to have undergone any significant transformation during the years before his first retirement. He was not substantially influenced by the scalar approach to improvisation followed by Miles Davis and others, but remained instead a "vertical" or chordal improviser. Except when he chose not to for shock value, his melodic lines seem guided by the underlying chord pattern. Although he does not faithfully articulate each chord as Coleman Hawkins might have done, harmonic outlines in the melodic lines are still very much in evidence.

Changes in melodic style

Following his two-year seclusion, ending in 1961, a noticeable change took place in his overall concept of jazz melody. The recordings *Our Man in Jazz* (RCA LPM 2612) and *Sonny Meets Hawk* (RCA LSP-2712) reveal a new direction in Rollins's melodic concept. No longer the thematic improviser, Rollins seems to have abandoned all of the goals and accomplishments of the late 1950s in favor of a more athematic approach, one apparently inspired by the then controversial saxophonist Ornette Coleman. Coleman, perhaps the most revolutionary figure of post-World War II jazz, strove for a style of improvisation known as "free jazz" in which preconceived harmonic progressions, themes, and structural formats played only a minimal role. The players improvised more or less spontaneously, supposedly without a preconceived plan or model, and therefore melodic, and harmonic agreement was often entirely accidental. Rollins's erratic solos on "Yesterdays" and "All the Things You Are," both from the latter album, reflect this tendency and form a marked contrast with the solos of the conservative but highly creative Coleman Hawkins on the same recording.

The reasons for Rollins's sudden abandonment of the "thematic" improvisation technique during the early 1960s seems related to an overall dissatisfaction with the current state of jazz improvisation that prompted his retirement in 1959, and will be explored in more detail below. Whatever the causes, the recordings made during 1962 and after reveal an entirely new direction in Rollins's playing, and with few exceptions he never again attempted to construct his melodic lines according to the principles of either thematic or motivic improvisation, the techniques that produced the great recordings of 1956—1959.

Rhythm

The rhythmic vocabulary of Sonny Rollins is founded upon the technical innovations of the bebop period of the late 1940s. This rhythmic style is distinguished by its greater emphasis on upbeats, irregular accent patterns, greater extremes in tempos, and a more dynamic sense of rhythmic swing. The melodic rhythm of virtually all modern jazz performers was affected by these changes, and by 1950 the short and sometimes mosaiclike phrases of swing and earlier jazz were gradually being replaced by a more rhythmically continuous melodic line, recognizable by its more frequent use of consecutive eighth-notes. This can easily be seen in the recordings of Gillespie, Parker, and others, whose melodic lines of moderate to fast tunes appear to be long, uninterrupted phrases of mostly eighth-note patterns. The continuous unbroken line was novel to the bebop style, and seems to have been the goal of the majority of jazz performers during this period, for the most significant challenge to every jazz player was in improvising over increasingly complex chord changes with as few pauses as possible. This demonstrated the player's familiarity with the tune and its harmony and his ability to shape melodic lines without interruption, in conformity with the underlying harmonies.

Melodic lines of consecutive eighth-notes remain evident in all postbebop performances; they constitute Rollins's basic and most fundamental rhythmic pattern and are present in the majority of his performances of medium to fast tunes. But while consecutive eighth-notes constitute a basic rhythmic pattern of all jazz after 1945, they were not always played with uniform evenness. At slow to medium tempos (to about $\quad = 90$), their execution varied between ♫♫♫ and ♪♪♪ . At faster tempos (to about $\quad = 180$) they were performed more consistently like triplets ♪♪♪♪♪♪; and only at tempos faster than $\quad = 180$ do they take on the even interpretation (♫♫♫♫♫♫) as notated. Transcriptions of jazz performances have traditionally not made these subtle rhythmic distinctions in the notation; therefore consecutive eighth-notes in the musical examples of this text are notated as "even" eighth-notes: their precise rhythmic interpretation can be inferred from the tempo.

In addition to varying the length of consecutive eighth-notes performed in this manner, it was customary to accent the "even numbered" notes of the pattern, thereby giving the melodic line a peculiar forward propulsion: the accent pattern ♫♫♫♫♫♫ , for example, has considerably more rhythmic momentum than the pattern ♫♫♫♫♫♫ . When the accenting of some even-numbered notes of a continuous eighth-note pattern coincided with the highest-sounding notes of the musical phrase, a remarkably syncopated melodic style resulted that contributed substantially to the feeling of modern swing. It was this style, first perfected on

recordings by Charlie Parker and Dizzy Gillespie, that was sub-
sequently adopted by all bop and postbop performers, including
Sonny Rollins.

Phrase construction

The phrase construction of bebop differs markedly from that of
earlier jazz. The phrases of the swing era were normally uniform in
length, usually four or eight measures, symmetrical in their relationship to one another, and generally followed the outline of the harmonic rhythm. Those of the late 1940s, however, were often of varying
lengths, beginning on a variety of beats in the measure, and not
necessarily guided by the harmonic rhythm of the model. Charlie
Parker's composition "Anthropology," for example, has an eight-bar
theme divided into five phrases, all starting at different points in the
measure, and examples of irregular phrasing in his improvised
choruses are even more abundant.

Rollins's phrase construction represents one of the most imaginative aspects of his playing and may be the most varied of any performer's of his time, including Charlie Parker. Position and length are
not controlled by the bar line, the harmonic rhythm, or, in some
cases, even the structure of the tune itself. Seldom is there any
consistent coincidence between the phrase lengths of Rollins's improvised choruses and those of the model. Nor is there any conformity to a uniform phrase length as there was in earlier jazz. Rollins
viewed melodic improvisation as a spontaneous form of expression,
employing primarily the harmonic framework of the model as the
basis for his improvisations. His phrases are of every imaginable
shape, form, and length from those constructed of two-note motives
("St. Thomas," I, 1—8)[2] to longer structures of irregular length, many
of which began at unpredictable points in the measure. There are
instances where phrases overlap ("Strode Rode," I, 9; "Surrey with the
Fringe on Top," III, 13) or anticipate the harmonic change ("Tune Up,"
I, 5). Some consist of rhythms in one note value only (in "I Feel a Song
Coming On," the bridge of the paraphrased chorus is made up of
single eighth-notes) and others consist of one pitch only ("Tune
Up," IV, 6—10). One of Rollins's most effective rhythmic devices
involves the repetition of brief motives on different beats of the mea-
sure. In "Little Folks," (I, 30—31), the motive |♫.♫♫♪| is imme-
diately sequenced and the rhythm changed to ♪|♫♫♫| in the next

measure. Other examples of rhythmic shifts can be found in "Pent Up House" (I, 25—28), "The Most Beautiful Girl" (I, 65—72), "Blue Seven" (VIII, 8—12; IX, 1—2), and "Lover" (I, 21—24).

Rollins deviates from the bebop pattern by separating his phrases with lengthy rests, some of them of several beats or more. This practice illustrates an important facet of his playing, that of using well-timed silence as a structural device to create tension and variety in the melodic line. By playing less continuously, and concentrating his ideas into briefer, more concise melodic units, Rollins achieved a more coherent melodic style, one devoid of extraneous "filler" material. The recordings "Blue Seven" and "Vierd Blues" are good examples of how the use of rests contributes to the overall effectiveness of the performance. Miles Davis was independently following the same course at about the same time, and his recordings from the mid-1950s also show an increasing use of long rests and simpler melodic lines. Both Davis and Rollins were reacting against the virtuosity of the bebop school, which produced a phrase structure and melodic rhythm of continuous complexity.

His use of "stop time" may also be related to the desire for simpler musical textures, and seems to be a preparation for the later practice of totally unaccompanied solos. (Stop time occurs when the rhythm section stops continuous play and punctuates only certain notes of the phrase, e.g., the first beat of every other measure.) The recordings "Just One of Those Things" (Emarcy MG 36098), "Dearly Beloved" and "The Last Time I Saw Paris" (both on Milestone 47007), and "I Know That You Know" (Verve 2683 054) contain segments in which Rollins plays with little accompaniment, a sure test of his rhythmic self-sufficiency, particularly in fast tempos.

Arhythmic groupings   Rollins employs a variety of phrasing techniques that defy accurate rhythmic transcription. In addition to the practice of "lagging behind" the beat, mentioned earlier, he occasionally divides the beat or measure into uneven rhythmic groupings, subdivisions that have no relationship to the underlying pulse of the meter. These notes are literally "squeezed" into a certain time interval (usually one to three beats) and cannot be transcribed into modern music notation. The third chorus of "Moritat" (III, 24—27), for example, contains measures of nine, ten, and eleven notes that are impossible to notate exactly. Numerous other examples exist of beat subdivisions into five and seven notes, and uneven groupings in the ballads are particularly frequent because of the greater rhythmic flexibility allowed by the slower tempos. Rollins's rhythmic interpretation of "Body and Soul" (Emarcy MG 36098) is so rhapsodic, for example, that a notationally accurate transcription of the cadenza at the end of his improvised chorus is largely conjectural. Jazz players refer to this as playing "outside" the meter and in most instances it is continued for brief periods only: but Rollins plays extended nonrhythmic sections for several measures or more. His recordings of "Pent Up House," "Tenor Madness," "Tune Up," and "Woodyn' You" all contain passages of such arhythmic playing.

New Meters

Finally, Rollins was among the first jazzmen to improvise extensively in triple meter. The use of meters other than duple or quadruple was not a common practice until the late 1950s, but Rollins's experiments with triple meter began as early as 1954 in collaboration with drummer Max Roach. His 1957 recording *Jazz in 3/4 Time* (Emarcy MG 36108), also with Roach, was the first jazz album consisting entirely of tunes in triple meter and anticipates the great interest in unusual meters among later jazz performers.

Rollins is as imaginative and creative in his rhythmic concepts as he is in his treatment of melody, but as a postbop jazz performer he followed the rhythmic innovations of Charlie Parker, Dizzy Gillespie, and Kenny Clarke, who initially broke away from the heavy downbeat orientation of the swing era. Rollins's rhythmic style of the late 1950s represents the next stage in the evolution of jazz rhythm, one without predictable patterns and formulae, but one that nevertheless lends much structural unity to the improvised lines. Although they never sound complicated or premeditated in their conception, Rollins's rhythmic patterns are, in fact, extremely varied and of great complexity, and contribute to the formal cohesiveness of the melodic line.

In contrast to the evolution of melody and rhythm, the harmonic language of jazz developed at a far slower pace. The chapter that follows will examine the state of jazz harmony at mid-century and the extent to which Sonny Rollins adapted this system in his music.

5

Harmony

Jazz Harmony
after World War II

By 1950, the harmonic vocabulary of contemporary jazz had developed into an identifiable system of chord progressions and chord types. The chords were grouped into three main categories: major chords (including the major seventh and the major triad with the added sixth); minor chords (including the minor seventh, the minor triad with an added sixth or major seventh, and the half-diminished seventh—actually a minor seventh with a flatted fifth), and dominant-seventh chords. All chords that were neither major nor minor functioned as dominant-seventh chords; this included all augmented and diminished chords (except for the half-diminished seventh). The chord categorization just described was the result of a long-evolving process and the combination of several harmonic systems: the basic tonal progressions (I, IV, and V) of the blues from the early jazz period; the chord types and progressions of popular music of the 1920s and after, principally those employing the II-V-I progression; a moderate use of late-nineteenth-century-style chromaticism, and extended tertial chords similar to those of French Impressionism. Some writers have suggested that post-World War II players owe their use of extended chords (ninths, elevenths and thirteenths) directly to the works of late-nineteenth-century and early-twentieth-century composers, particularly the French Impressionists. While it isn't surprising that these musicians were acquainted with blues progressions of earlier jazz and the harmonic progressions of popular music of the 1920s and 1930s, it is highly unlikely that the jazz players of this time were familiar with the works of European composers. A more likely explanation is that their use of extended chords is the logical result of their search for more complex harmonic materials as a basis for their improvisations.

The Blues

The blues, by far the most common harmonic model used by jazz performers of the 1940s, consisted originally of a very simple harmonic formula (there is no standard blues melody) of twelve or less often sixteen measures, employing the tonic, subdominant, and dominant chords in the following sequence (see example 5).

Example 5. Early blues progression[1]

This was the basic pattern used during the late-nineteenth century and for the entire period of "Ragtime" and early jazz. During the late 1930s, some other chords were added to the basic formula, producing a faster harmonic rhythm, so that the final result resembled the following scheme (see example 6).

Example 6. Blues progression of the Swing Era

The most significant changes in the simple blues pattern came in the late 1940s with the use of extended chords (see example 7).

Example 7. Blues progression, circa 1950

Popular songs

After the blues, the next most commonly used harmonic source for jazz improvisation during this period was the popular song. Originating in either a Broadway musical, a vaudeville show, a film, or less often as an independently composed tune, the popular song was familiar to large numbers of jazz musicians as well as the American public. Its harmonic structure, the result of frequent shifts to temporary key centers and the liberal use of altered chords built on chromatic degrees of the scale, provided the jazz improviser with harmonic resources that could not be found in any other kind of folk or "ethnic" music. The popular song provided a rich and varied resource for the jazz musician, and native American and European folk songs were relatively simple by comparison. The latter were frequently conceived as a result of the "oral" tradition and their melodic and harmonic structure necessarily required simplicity as it was transmitted from one generation to the next. But many American popular songs were written by trained composers, such as Harold Arlen, Cole Porter, Richard Rodgers, and George Gershwin; their music was generally more sophisticated and more resourceful than simpler song types.

The vast majority of popular songs used for this purpose were written in major keys, but, except for beginnings and endings, the original key signature had little to do with the subsequent chord progressions of the tune. Modulation and, more often, abrupt

changes to distantly related keys were commonplace as was the use
of nonresolving "temporary" dominants, i.e., dominant-seventh
chords, constructed on any degree or altered degree of the scale, that
do not resolve to their natural tonics. This combination of functional
and nonfunctional chords became a feature of a large number of
popular songs, and the sudden shifts of tonal centers that resulted
from this mixture produced harmonic goals of relatively brief duration (see example 8).

Example 8. "Sophisticated Lady" (Duke Ellington)

Harmonic patterns as mobile as this one would seem to present a
considerable challenge to the jazz musician, who must learn by
memory a large number of tunes, but, in fact, some repetitious
patterns do occur. The most constant progression present in
virtually all popular songs is the II-V-I or the II-V (the I chord is
sometimes omitted), the basic chord sequence of all functional harmony. This progression, often appearing in the context of a circle of
fifths, lends a sense of direction to what in the popular song would
otherwise be an extremely variable and unstable series of chord
progressions. As the most fundamental progression within jazz, the
II—V—I sequence became the progression most often encountered
by the improvising jazz musician, and therefore the basic formula to
be mastered when improvising on a standard popular tune.

Chord substitution

In their improvisations, jazz performers have rarely been content to
use the harmonies of the standard model as originally published; the
chordal accompaniments of the tunes, therefore, were frequently
expanded by the use of "extended" chords[2] and by chord substitution. The substitution principle was widely employed in post-World
War II jazz as a means of providing color within the harmonic phrase

and also as a challenge to the improvising jazz player, who shaped his melodic lines in conformity with the new sonorities. The practice of chord substitution began as players tired of playing tunes with a limited number of chord changes, or with the same pattern of chord changes (many popular tunes of this time followed a similar chord sequence). Chord substitution entails the replacement of a standard chord used to harmonize a popular tune with another (usually more colorful) chord. The large variety of these chords, and particularly the theories governing their use, developed into a theoretical system of some complexity. Some theorists have cautioned against the exaggerated emphasis given to the role of chord substitutions in jazz, but there can be no doubt that it was a factor in the melodic line construction of many important jazz performers, including Rollins.

Substitutions were most often devised for the dominant-seventh chord, a common alternative being another dominant-seventh chord constructed on the note a tritone away. Following this rule, a B^7 chord could be substituted for an F^7 chord without disturbing the harmonic function of the progression. The normal resolution of the F^7 chord would be to Bb and therefore the B^7 chord functions as a bII^7—a modern adaptation of what traditional theorists have labeled the "Neapolitan sixth." Appropriate substitutions for the other chord types were constructed according to the context in which they were used (i.e., their position in the progression) and also according to their agreement with the melody note sounding at that time.

Rollins's Contributions

The harmonic style of Sonny Rollins may be the least innovative aspect of his improvisations. By the time his professional career began in the early 1950s, the harmonic practices described above had become well entrenched in the jazzman's vocabulary. Rollins added very little to the basic harmonic repertoire of chord types; his compositions of this period ("Blue Seven," "Pent Up House," "Doxy," "Tenor Madness," etc.) reveal a simple harmonic style—one very much unlike that of the bebop era. But when improvising, he found imaginative ways in which to shape his melodic lines using the chords of the model as a harmonic foundation. The examination of the harmonic aspects of Rollins's music will therefore center upon the relationship of the improvised melodic line and the supporting harmony. The fundamental question to be answered is: to what extent do the notes of Rollins's improvised melody agree with the harmonies of the model?

Theorists in the past have generally assumed that the coincidence between improvised melody and the harmonic framework was either necessarily very close or that nonchordal tones could somehow be explained according to the traditional principles governing the resolution of dissonances: "In jazz the improvised melodic line and the chords from which it originates are indissolubly bound together. The pitches that form the improvised line are either members of the chords that accompany them, or they are dissonant pitches, subject to the laws of functional harmony that regulate the use and placement of dissonances."[3]

At best, this view represents an ideal of near total conformity between improvised melody and harmonic foundation of a tune, but even in early jazz, where the harmonic progressions of the models were comparatively simple, this was often not the case. Recent studies show a high incidence of harmonic disagreement in early jazz between the improvising soloist and the piano, bass, and other chordal instruments supplying the harmonic background. Gunther Schuller, for example, speaks of "thousands" of such harmonic discrepancies, and names even so accomplished a group as the Creole Jazz Band, led by King Oliver, as being guilty of such flaws. These were largely unintentional, of course, and resulted from the incompetence of the soloists, accompanists, or both.[4] With the expanded harmonies of modern jazz, the relationship of the improvised melody and harmonic background became even more strained, not because of player errors but because the threshold of dissonance had been increased considerably.

Use of dissonance

The improvisations of Rollins show at least three different levels of coincidence between melody and harmony. There are some passages where the melodic line adheres very closely to the supporting chords; a second harmonic level where the improvised line contains a few chordal tones, with the remaining notes accountable for as "extended chordal tones" or traditional nonharmonic tones; and a third harmonic texture in which the upper chord extension and the chromatic alterations are used to such a degree, that the melody appears totally foreign to the harmonies of the model.

Instances of close harmonic agreement are fairly numerous in Rollins's recordings. On occasion he arpeggiates a chord so that the agreement is obvious, but more often the melody is formed from the scale implied by the chord progression (see examples 9 and 10).

Example 9. "St. Thomas," III, 3—5

Example 10. "Strode Rode," I, 25—27

In the above examples, the three chords of each belong to the keys of C major and Ab major, respectively, and Rollins's melodies clearly lie within those harmonic frameworks. When chords are used that belong to more than one key, Rollins adjusts his melodic line so as to agree with the changes of harmony (see example 11).

Example 11. "Little Folks," II, 7—9

Occasionally Rollins avoids the notes of the basic chord (root, third, fifth, and seventh) and forms his melodic lines from the notes of the extension (ninths, elevenths, and thirteenths). When this occurs, the simultaneous sounding of the basic chords by the accompaniment and Rollins's melody produce a cumulative effect of polychordal harmony (see example 12).

Example 12. "Blue Seven," II, 8—11

By far the most striking melodic passages, however, are those in which the emphasis of the extended chord tones and their chromatic alterations is so strong that they sound of a different tonal area and cannot be fully accounted for by any of the previous explanations (see example 13). Known as "playing outside" the harmonic framework when the clashes become extreme, this practice first occurred in the late 1940s and became more frequent in the 1960s and 1970s. When used sparingly, it creates a great harmonic "coloring" effect, usually passing so quickly that the listener has little chance to perceive the inherent dissonance. Other instances of harmonic conflict are the result of chord anticipations where the melody anticipates the next harmonic change. "Little Folks," for example, has the outline of a Bb augmented chord appearing one measure early against an Ab seventh chord (see example 38, I, 31). Passing chords are also used extensively, as are a variety of bitonal devices exploiting the augmented-fourth or diminished-fifth relationship.

Example 13. "Tune Up," III, 30—32

Tritone relationships

Rollins's use of the tritone constitutes an important feature of his harmonic style, and examples can be found in a relatively large number of his recorded performances, especially those with blues structure. Perhaps inspired by Thelonious Monk's frequent use of them in his early compositions, the tritone becomes Rollins's favorite dissonance and is present on three different structural levels within his performances: first, as a melodic interval; next, as the basis for a whole-tone scale pattern; and finally, as the intervallic distance between two keys.

Two of these three levels are present in Rollins's 1956 recording of "Blue Seven." The theme of "Blue Seven" begins with a tritone (D—Ab) and this melodic interval is prominently used throughout each improvised chorus. When the harmony changes to the subdominant (measures 5—6 of each chorus) the presence of the tritone is continued with the augmented triad Db, F, A. So consistent is

Rollins's use of this device that this chord is implied in the fifth and sixth measures of every improvised chorus except three (choruses III, VIII, and IX). The essential notes of the theme (D, E, Ab), which are also the third, flatted-fifth, and seventh of the Bb dominant chord, respectively, may also be seen in the enharmonic spelling (E, G#, D) as outlining the E dominant-seventh chord, therefore suggesting an additional tritone relationship with the key of Bb. Bitonality is also a factor in the earlier recording of "Vierd Blues," although to a lesser degree. Here the tritone appears only sporadically as a melodic interval (see II, 1; III, 5) but the overall character of Rollins's solo on this tune is so similar that "Vierd Blues" might be regarded as a predecessor of "Blue Seven."[5]

Whole-tone and diminished scales

The tritone interval when used melodically is related to two important scale types: the whole-tone scale and the diminished scale, both of which figure prominently in Rollins's harmonic thinking.

Whole-tone scales usually appear as broken melodic figures, rarely in clear scale patterns, and they are frequently used in conjunction with dominant-seventh chords. The origin of their use in jazz is difficult to determine, but their presence is implied, at least, in the compositions of Thelonious Monk from the early 1940s.

Diminished scales have only recently been identified by theorists as recognizable musical structures in jazz improvisation, and Rollins may well be the first jazz artist to make extensive use of these structures. The scale comes in several versions, its structure being determined by the type of chord sounding in the harmony at the time; the notes of the scale must agree with the notes of the diminished chord that it is accompanying. The diminished scale consisting of alternate half- and whole-steps (example 14) is known as the "half-step/whole-step" diminished scale, and the scale consist-

Example 14. Half-step/Whole-step Diminished Scale

ing of the opposite arrangement is known as the "whole-step/half-step" diminished scale (example 15). A third type is called the "half-diminished" scale (the notes of the scale include all the notes of the

Example 15. Whole-step/Half-step Diminished Scale

diminished-seventh or half diminished-seventh chord, hence the name) or the diminished "whole-tone" scale, because of the four whole-steps between the last five notes (example 16).

Example 16. Diminished Whole-tone Scale

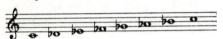

Diminished scales account for a significant proportion of the chromatic passages in Rollins's music, especially those harmonized by half-diminished-seventh chords or dominant-seventh chords with altered ninths, and his early use of these may constitute one of his most original contributions to jazz harmony. The passage quoted in example 17 illustrates a clear instance of the "whole-step/half-step" diminished scale. The first phrase (measures 25—26) consists of such a scale on G, and the second phrase (measures 27—28) is composed of an identical scale on F.

Example 17. "Woodyn' You," I, 25—28

Rollins effectively uses the diminished scale when improvising over the "bII chord substitution" discussed earlier. The two structures, in fact, can be seen to be one and the same, since the notes of the bII⁷ substitute chord are contained within the diminished scale of the original dominant (see example 18).

Example 18. Half-step/Whole-step Diminished Scale on G(G⁷); bII(Db⁷)

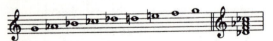

In this context, the diminished scale provides a smooth transition from the last measure(s) of one chorus or phrase to the first measure of the next and adds to the overall continuity of Rollins's melodic lines (example 19).[6]

Example 19. "Vierd Blues," IV, 12

It's unlikely, of course, that Rollins was aware of the theory of diminished scales and the likelihood is that he used them unconsciously; but the example above illustrates how close this one-measure run comes to the theoretical structure built on F: of the fifteen notes in this descending passage, only three (Bb, Fb and G) do not appear in the F half-step/whole-step diminished scale.

Two remaining harmonic patterns or formulae appear with some consistency in Rollins's work and deserve special mention: the skillful improvisations on the II—V—I progression and the use of the "Blues Scale."

The II—V—I progression

Rollins recorded many popular standards and original jazz tunes during the years 1949—1962, and the II—V or II—V—I progression is the most frequently encountered chord sequence within these tune types. His improvised melodic lines based on these chord changes reveal an extremely fertile imagination and one capable of producing melodic lines of great continuity. So smooth is his linking of one melodic idea with another that many appear to flow logically one from another in seamless fashion and in close conformity with the supporting chord progressions (see examples 20—22).

Example 20. "Pent Up House," II, 27—30

Example 21. "Woodyn' You," I, 9—12

Example 22. "Tune Up," I, 17—20

The Blues scale

The blues scale consists of the tonic, the flatted third, the fourth, the augmented fourth, the fifth, and the flatted seventh degrees of the major scale (see example 23).

Example 23. Blues Scale on C

As one of the fundamental structures of the bebop period, the blues scale had become something of a cliché by the mid-1950s. Rollins employed it principally in the performance of blues tunes, but he was always careful to disguise its appearance by fragmenting it and avoiding its use as an unaltered scale (see examples 24 and 25).

Example 24. "Vierd Blues," IV, 6—7 (Based on the Bb Blues Scale)

Example 25. "Blue Seven," V, 5—7 (Based on the Bb Blues Scale)

Rollins's achievements in the use of harmonic resources are modest when compared to the formal aspects of his playing. Charlie Parker and his contemporaries of a few years before had laid the groundwork for the use of extended chords, an elaborate scheme of chord substitutions, and the richer and more varied harmonic progressions in their original jazz compositions. Rollins borrowed much of what they accomplished and incorporated it into his own playing. Even his experiments with the tritone and bitonality, both relatively novel concepts to jazz harmony, represent an expansion of tertial harmony rather than the creation of new sonorities. But while he used harmonic structures introduced by others, he assimilated them into his personal style. His harmonic vocabulary appears deceptively simple, when he confines his playing to the normal chord limits, and yet his bold use of the chromatically altered notes of the extensions in shaping melodies clearly distinguishes him from the other jazz performers of this era. Phrases containing large numbers of foreign tones against the supporting harmony are fairly numerous in the recordings, but the dissonance appears harmonically unified with the remainder of the improvisation because of the rhythmic momentum of the melodic lines and the manner in which he links phrases thematically. Most important of all, his improvising over fixed harmonic changes never sounds contrived or premeditated, for Rollins was concerned foremost with playing melodies, and the chord progression was merely the substratum upon which they were constructed.

6

Form and Structure

Jazz until 1955
Some Problems and Solutions

Melody, rhythm, and harmony, normally the most readily identifiable attributes of any music, are comparatively easy concepts to understand about jazz compared to the more subtle aspect of formal organization. As a result form and structure played only a minor role in jazz until the early 1950s. Jazz rhythm, melody, and harmony had all undergone significant transformations in the fifty years or more of jazz's existence, but there was little concern shown for formal organization in the jazz performance. Abrupt or disorganized starts, truncated endings, and ensemble portions incongruous with the overall formal structure of the performance were often the rule in early jazz. Although much of this was refined during the 1930s and 1940s as the players grew more musically sophisticated, the problem of melodic continuity still remained in the improvised choruses. To some extent this is understandable, for the very act of improvising does not encourage preconceived formal and structural planning. Players were concerned more with the immediate significance of what they were playing and did not consider the overall cohesiveness of an improvised performance. More often than not even the most inspired improvisations were melodically episodic and lacked a sense of goal or direction.

Evidence of structural uniformity was also lacking on other levels, particularly between the improvisations of one soloist and that of another within the same performance. Each player was expected to contribute something unique, something especially his own, and thus little effort was made to relate one performer's improvisation with the one that preceded him. But while the individuality and spontaneity of the jazz solo were preserved in this manner, most improvisations achieved only momentary significance and any sense of overall unity was generally lost. This last point is important, because some semblance of cohesive development is really what separates a truly outstanding melodic improvisation from an average one.

The various styles of jazz were affected differently by the presence or absence of melodic development within the improvised sections. The lack of unity in early jazz, for example, did not necessarily have an adverse affect on the performance because the melodic and harmonic resources of the majority of early jazz tunes were simple enough so that the music could succeed on the basis of its rhythmic vitality alone. This is borne out by the performances of early jazz's most important soloist, Louis Armstrong, whose solos are the epitome of the simple, direct, declarative style based on a minimum of chords and chord types. As jazz tunes grew more complex, however, and the harmonic, rhythmic, and melodic resources more heterogeneous, jazz performers felt a need to organize their improvisations into more meaningful musical statements. By 1950, the improvised material found in a typical jazz performance could be classified into several distinct types or melodic styles.

Types of improvised material

"Running the changes"   By far the greatest proportion of time in the improvised solo was taken up with the player's "running the changes." The melodic lines of such sections may have conformed closely to the supporting harmonies but usually contained few clearly defined melodic ideas and functioned more as passages of "filler material," connecting one melodic idea or inspiration with the next. The average jazz improviser may have employed this method almost exclusively, his solos being a string of nonthematic figures that changed with the harmonic progression. This was the predominant improvisatory technique of the 1940s, a continuous but abstract melodic style, whose objective was to demonstrate the performer's ability to improvise on rapidly moving chord changes. The disadvantages of such a technique, however, are that no recognizable melodic development takes place within the improvisation, and the solo, usually a succession of unrelated ideas, often becomes tiring for the listener. This partially explains the failure of bebop as a "popular" style of jazz. As with popular music, a particular style of jazz succeeds because it is tuneful and its melodies are easily remembered.

Theme references and quotations   A contrasting type of improvised material made use of references to the theme of the model, or of interpolations of extraneous melodic material. The creative performer resorted to quoting the theme only rarely in the course of his improvisation; his objective was not to restate the theme but to develop new thematic interest. If the improvisation was particularly complex harmonically or melodically, however, an occasional reference to the theme aided the other performers and listeners in following its progress. The theme of the model continued to be paraphrased, of course, at the beginning and end of all performances, as part of an overall three-sectional performance scheme (paraphrase/improvisation/paraphrase).

The quotation of unrelated themes was another matter entirely, and occurred frequently in jazz of the 1940s and 1950s. Such quotations were normally of familiar (although irrelevant) material. When they functioned as humorous alternatives to the creation of original melodic ideas, they ultimately detracted from the overall unity of the improvisation, and by the late 1950s the practice was no longer fashionable.

Signs of unity: motives and sequences   The lack of cohesion in the jazz solo was eased somewhat as players unconsciously began to use recurring motives in their improvisations. In his study of Charlie Parker, Owens tabulates approximately one hundred such motives in Parker's improvisations, categorizing them according to shape, frequency of use, and application.[1] It is important to recognize, however, that in jazz performances these motives are not employed in the same manner as in composed music, since they rarely undergo any development within the course of the improvisation. Instead, they merely "recur" from time to time, giving just the "appearance" of some formal organization. Jazz authors in the past have frequently failed to make this clear in their writings. The term "motive" is actually a misnomer, since more often than not no true motivic development takes place. (Rollins's performances of "Blue Seven" and "St. Thomas," discussed later, may be rare exceptions to this general rule.)

Other devices contributing to the structural integrity of the jazz performance include various repetition schemes, particularly those employing the sequence. Melodic sequences had been used occasionally in traditional jazz, but in jazz after World War II they are quite common (see example 26).

Example 26. Bill Evans, "Speak Low," (Weill), Riverside RLP—12—223, 9—16

The mid-1950s

Thus the jazz performer, by the very fact that he was improvising, was faced with a seemingly insurmountable task: to be spontaneous and still create coherent, unified melody at one and the same time. This difficulty challenged every jazz player, and yet, even at the time of Charlie Parker's death (1955) no performer had demonstrated an effective solution.

Parker the brilliant technician and master improviser may have overcome the problem himself had he lived longer; however, in the vast majority of his recordings, he appears indifferent to the overall form of his improvisations. There are some notable exceptions: "Embraceable You" (Dial 1024), in which he never states Gershwin's melody, but creates a tightly knit improvisation beginning with a six-note motive which he then sequences melodically. But even in his best performances (Ko-Ko, "Cool Blues," "Ornithology," "Donna Lee," and many more) Parker is essentially an "episodic" jazz performer who improvised brilliantly on the harmonic materials at hand but felt little need to connect his ideas into unified melodic statements.

Other styles of jazz concurrent with the end of the bebop era show even less awareness of the problems facing jazz improvisation. The so-called "cool" style of the 1950s, for example, was one that minimized the role of improvisation by shifting the emphasis to the fixed portions of the music. Most of the advances in this style, therefore, occurred in the areas of jazz "composition," arranging and instrumentation. Since melodic improvisation ceased to be the central core of the jazz performance, it is not surprising that for all the commercial success that cool jazz enjoyed, the "West Coast" school did not produce a single melodic improviser of the first rank. (One possible exception may be alto saxophonist Paul Desmond, who performed with the Dave Brubeck Quartet. Desmond's 1954 recording of "Audrey" [Columbia CL-622] is an impressive example of thematic improvisation in the West Coast style.)

Thus significant improvements were needed in the form and structure of jazz after World War II. Although not clearly recognized as such by the performers themselves, most of the technical advancements of the preceding eras represented a groping for greater unification of ideas in the improvised sections.

Sonny Rollins: Structural Unity in the Improvised Line

Sonny Rollins appears to have been aware of the challenge of improvising melodically from the very start of his professional career. Even in the early recordings with Miles Davis in 1951 and again in 1954, Rollins stands in bold relief to the other improvisers in the ensemble. His melodic ideas unfold in a natural sequence, one leading logically to the next, and nonmelodic passages are kept to a minimum as are outright references to the theme. Rollins's improvisation in the 1954 recording of "But Not for Me," for example, begins with a clear melodic idea (mm. 1—4) which is immediately answered (mm. 5—8) (see example 27). The process is repeated again with a new melodic idea (mm. 16—19) and its subsequent continuation (mm. 20—24) (see example 28).

Example 27. "But Not for Me," meas. 1—8

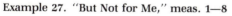

Example 28. "But Not for Me," meas. 16—24

Although melodic continuity is maintained for a total of only sixteen measures (half of the 32-measure first chorus), the passages above were still unique when one considers that the percentage of melodically unified passages by other players—even the most skilled improvisers—was usually far less.

Rollins's phrase structure and rhythmic conception in these early recordings are still very conventional, however; phrases closely follow the two- and four-measure margins of the original tune, and the rhythmic figures are predominantly the eighth-note and triplet patterns so firmly established by the bebop style. But in every other respect, these early recordings reveal Rollins as a performer with a promising new method of improvising jazz, one that has as its goal a form of thematic development.

Rollins perfected his improvisatory technique, including his method of "thematic improvising" (a term first used by Gunther Schuller), between the years 1956 and 1959. A large proportion of his performances recorded during this time exhibit some evidence of melodic continuity in the improvised sections. Moreover, a close look at the techniques employed show that his improvisations may be divided into three distinct categories: improvisations resulting from motivic development; those resulting from thematic development; and those exhibiting a combination of these two approaches. Less distinct fourth and fifth categories may be added to account for the improvisations that do not completely conform to any of the above classifications. One group contains neither themes nor motives but exhibits a nonthematic technique generated by the chord changes. A separate but related group has recognizable motives interspersed throughout the figuration, but they undergo no true development. These categories are not mutually exclusive and some performances exhibit combinations of three or more techniques. Rollins's improvisation on "Wagon Wheels," for example, is primarily thematic in its organization, but also contains some nonmelodic ("change running") sections. "Little Folks" (see example 38) exhibits a clear motivic organization, but also has an extended section of nonmelodic or "filler" figuration (I, 17—29).

Nonthematic improvisations

Rollins's improvisations on "But Not for Me," "Misterioso," and "Woodyn' You" comprise the group based on nonthematic figuration, i.e., they contain neither clearly recognizable themes nor motives. As a young performer, Rollins mastered this technique first; it had been one of the established methods of improvisation by the outstanding performers of the bebop era, performers whom Rollins admired and who had a profound influence on his early career. "Woodyn' You" and "Misterioso" are particularly clear illustrations of this technique. In the former, the melodic line is nearly continuous (only brief rests) and is surprisingly unified despite the paucity of tuneful melodic ideas. This performance demonstrates Rollins's ability to create an abstract melodic line that is self-perpetuating. With the exception of the sequences in the first chorus (I, 5—7, 21—22, 25—28), no other repetitive devices occur; the melodic line is formed instead by an additive process, each phrase growing out of the previous one.

The 1957 recording of "Misterioso" is similarly lacking in distinct melodic ideas and consists only of unrelated groupings of figures separated by lengthy rests. Although expertly performed by Rollins, this improvisation is an "of the moment" extemporization gaining its continuity and forward propulsion from Rollins's extraordinary rhythmic thrust and skillful treatment of the Bb blues scale.

Figuration

A related group of tunes employs figuration with occasional references to distinct motives or melodic fragments. "I Feel a Song Coming On," "I Mean You," "Lover," "Moritat," "Strode Rode," and "Vierd Blues" fall into this category. In "I Feel a Song Coming On," what would otherwise be a pure example of non thematic improvisation over the chord changes is interrupted twice by lyrical passages derived from a motive of the original theme. (Compare example 29 with a passage of the original theme [example 30].)

Example 29. "I Feel a Song Coming On," 54—57

Example 30. "I Feel a Song Coming On," 3—5

A similar procedure is followed in "I Mean You." A brief melodic fragment outlining the F-major triad and derived from the first two measures of the original theme is heard on two other occasions in the course of the improvisation (I, 19—20 and 33—34). Again these references to a motive do not constitute actual motivic development since they are quoted more or less intact. Instead they function as unifying fragments linking the diverse and complicated improvisation with material of the original model.

Motivic development

In "Strode Rode" Rollins begins his improvisation with a motive (example 31) taken from a portion of the theme (example 32).

Example 31. "Strode Rode," I, 1—3

Example 32. "Strode Rode," 10—11

A second melodic fragment (example 33) is introduced eight measures later and reappears a total of ten times throughout the improvisation.

Example 33. "Strode Rode" I, 11

While the motive itself undergoes no true development during this time, the principal note (D-natural) becomes the subject of an eight-measure episode (I, 29—36).

Rollins's reasons for employing motives in this manner are not entirely clear, since they interrupt the otherwise uniform sections of nonthematic improvisation. Given the abstract nature of the improvisation in this performance, however, the purpose may have been to maintain some identification with the original theme.

Rollins's 1956 recording of his own composition "Blue Seven" is the most compactly organized of the performances exhibiting motivic construction; it is also, because of Schuller's aforementioned analysis of it in the *Jazz Review*, Rollins's most thoroughly studied performance to date. Schuller identifies seven distinct motives in this recording and observes that Rollins's improvisation is so well unified that of the twenty-eight measures he plays in his eleventh through thirteenth choruses, only six are not directly related to the melodic material of the opening measures. Schuller concludes that the resulting unity could be achieved by a composer who spent days or weeks perfecting a passage, but that it is a considerable accomplishment in the context of a spontaneous jazz performance.[2] "Blue Seven" contains examples of true motivic development, rather than mere repetition. The next two examples, for instance, illustrate how one of the principal motives (example 34) is transformed through diminution (example 35). The transformed version (example 35) is then repeated

Example 34. "Blue Seven," 2—3

Example 35. "Blue Seven," VIII, 8—9

five times, the first three repetitions on different beats within the measure (VIII, 8—12; IX, 1—3).

Later an important interval (the half-step, G—Ab) contained in the original motive (example 34) becomes the subject of an episode when it is inverted to a major seventh (example 36).

Example 36. "Blue Seven," XIII, 4—7

Another recorded performance exhibiting a tightly organized motive structure is the 1956 recording of "St. Thomas" (see example 37). The first chorus of this improvisation consists almost entirely of the development of the two-note motive G—C (an inversion of the first two notes of the theme). In the course of its development, Rollins shifts its placement in the measure, so that it eventually falls on every strong beat; he further varies the size of the original from a perfect fifth to a major second, and every interval in between: diminished fifth, perfect fourth, major third, and minor third (example 37, I, 1—21). The remaining choruses contain a mixture of material developed both motivically and thematically. The first eight measures of the second chorus, for example, utilize material from the theme itself, so that the result is a new (although related) theme. Throughout the improvised choruses that follow there are many thematic sections separating the nonthematic figuration (mostly eighth-note figures), and all the former bear an unmistakable resemblance to portions of the original theme.

The 1957 recording of "Little Folks" is peculiar for its unusually long episode sequentially developed from a single motive (see example 38, I, 2). The motive is later transformed into one of Rollins's favorite figures, the gruppetto ♪♫ , discussed earlier, and Rollins actually carries the development of this motive to the extreme by sequencing it in almost every measure (eleven in all out of the first sixteen measures) (I, 2—16). Examples of the same motive can be found in other performances: "Blue Seven," "Lover," "Misterioso" (appears in half-values ♫ , "Moritat," "The Most Beautiful Girl in the World," "Wagon Wheels," and "The Surrey with the Fringe on the Top."

Example 37. "St. Thomas," I, 1—32

Example 38. "Little Folks," I, 1—32

New themes

Rollins was not the first performer to use motives as a structural aid
in his improvisations. Other players had done so before, but he may
be the first to have expanded his improvisations by the creation of
new themes, themes that further develop the thematic material of
the original model. "Body and Soul," "The Most Beautiful Girl," "Pent
Up House," "Wagon Wheels," and "Without a Song" all contain passages of such "thematic" improvisation.

In the "Body and Soul" recording, no doubt inspired by Coleman
Hawkins's famous recording of 1939, Rollins begins by closely paraphrasing the melody for the first eight measures before creating a
new theme, which, although close to the original, is different enough
to suggest a true "thematic variation." A lesser performer may have
been content to improvise on the chord changes at this point, but
Rollins develops the original theme of the model, so that the second
eight measures of the improvisation (mm. 9—16) lead very naturally
to the change of key (m. 17). When he plays again in the last eight
measures of the second chorus, his variation is elaborate enough (see
example 40) to constitute an entirely new theme.

Rollins's method of generating a thematic improvisation varies
from performance to performance, but the principal technique used
in "Body and Soul" is the melodic sequence. Example 39 shows how
a motive (marked in brackets) derived from the original melody is
developed by sequence to form a thematically related episode. (The
characteristic feature of the motive is the large leap (G—Ab), which is
also a prominent characteristic of the tune's theme.

Example 39. "Body and Soul," 14—16

Sequence is also used by Rollins in the last chorus to extend a new
melodic idea whose shape is intervallically related to the original
theme (see example 40).

Example 40. "Body and Soul," II, 25—26

Rollins's performance of "The Most Beautiful Girl in the World" is another remarkably unified improvisation, demonstrating his ability to improvise thematically on material from the original tune. Here the connecting motive derived from the model is not as direct as it was in "Body and Soul" (example 40), but Rollins nevertheless develops a melodic line of great cohesion that continues without interruption for thirty-two measures (example 41).

"Wagon Wheels" illustrates how good thematic use can be made of what would ordinarily be considered a very dull theme. Rollins begins improvising thematically with the four-measure break before the first chorus. The next eight measures form a thematic improvisation based on segments of the model's theme. In the process, he introduces brief melodic ideas that resemble key motives of the original melody. This differs from simple paraphrasing since the improvised sections are not always derived from corresponding parts of the theme.

A similar procedure is followed in the third improvised chorus of "Moritat," where Rollins improvises a nearly continuous melodic line for the first twenty-three measures. Unlike the previous example, however, the improvisation and the theme are related not by motives but only by a general similarity in sound. One, in fact, could play both the original theme and the third chorus of Rollins's improvisation simultaneously and the two would complement each other perfectly, Rollins's improvisation forming a compatible counterline to the original.

The 1962 recording of "Without a Song" is the most economical of all Rollins's thematic improvisations, for it is based on only one note. In this performance, Rollins reduces Vincent Youman's melody to its most basic tone, Eb, the tonic of the key; this single tone then becomes the fulcrum for a thematic improvisation that (except for the interruptions of the guitar solo, I, 33—39) extends for the entire first chorus. By keeping the Eb as the center tone of his improvisation, Rollins demonstrates his ability to develop an imaginative extemporization based on extremely limited resources.

Example 41. "The Most Beautiful Girl in the World," I, 1—32

Thematic and motivic

Other important recordings from this period ("The Surrey with the Fringe on the Top," "Tenor Madness," and "Tune Up") contain elements of both thematic and motivic improvisation.

"Tune Up" makes an obvious use of motives, since Rollins begins the improvisation with a clear melodic idea (example 42) that expands into a complete phrase (I, 1—4) before being repeated twice sequentially (I, 5—8 and I, 9—12).

Example 42. "Tune Up," I, 1—2

The first four measures of the second chorus begin with a different motive (example 43), which is developed briefly for eight measures (II, 1—8) before becoming the basis for an extended development in the fourth chorus (IV, 5—24).

Example 43. "Tune Up," II, 1—2

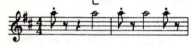

Between the appearances of these contrasting motives, several brief lyrical themes occur, which are easily distinguished from the remainder of the improvisation and which resemble the original theme because of their lengthened note values and legato phrasing.

Rollins's improvisation on the blues tune "Tenor Madness" follows a procedure similar to that used in "Tune Up." After beginning his first improvised chorus with a motive inspired by the first two notes of the theme, he then launches into an eight-chorus improvisation consisting primarily of an athematic improvisation that is interrupted from time to time by lyrical melodic passages. These passages are thematically related to the original melody and serve to unify the lengthy improvisation.

Thus Rollins freely mixes his improvisatory techniques, sometimes employing one more than another but never restricting his improvisations to only one method within the same performance. His solution to improvisation is as spontaneous as that of any performer of his time or before, and later recordings of some of the tunes discussed show divergent approaches in their formal organization. Similarly, his accomplishments in maintaining a sense of unity within the improvisation were never the result of any deliberate motivic or thematic construction, for with all the inspired playing present in his solos, there is enough imperfection to indicate that Rollins was truly spontaneous. His quotation of unrelated melodic material (as, for example, "The Irish Washerwoman" in "Far Out East" [Verve V-68430], the bugle fanfare in "But Not For Me" [III, 30—31], or the forced quotation of "Without a Song" in the fourth chorus of "Four" [RCA LPM-2927]) and his repertoire of staccato honks and growls, which sometimes interrupt an otherwise unified performance, further indicate that Rollins's improvisations lacked preconceived planning. It is this quality of spontaneity together with an instinct for structural integrity that clearly separate Rollins's improvisations from those of other performers of his generation. His best performances were spontaneous, but at the same time they revealed logical formal development.

Toward a new era

Sonny Rollins's remarkable achievements as a melodic improviser coincided almost as if by accident with the demise of an era. The postbop period was in a state of decline in the late 1950s, and the break that was to come in the 1960s ushered in some of the most sudden and drastic changes ever in the history of jazz. Uncomfortable in his role as a leading jazz improviser, Rollins needed time to catch up musically and adjust to the change. This he did in the fall of 1959, by voluntarily withdrawing from public appearances. Chapters 7 through 9 of this book will examine the major changes affecting the jazz of the 1960s and 1970s and investigate the manner in which Sonny Rollins responded to this new music.

7

The New Jazz
of the 1960s

When Sonny Rollins embarked on his self-imposed sabbatical in the fall of 1959 little did he realize the sweeping changes that would affect jazz in the years to come. With few exceptions the evolution of jazz had been an orderly procedure, passing easily from one generation or style to the next. There were some exceptions: the experiments of Charlie Parker and Dizzy Gillespie of the early 1940s and the subsequent controversy surrounding bebop. Certainly the idea of performing a more challenging repertoire of nondanceable jazz tunes seemed revolutionary at the time. But seen in retrospect, bebop resulted in an enrichment of the older system; an expansion of its harmonic, rhythmic, and melodic resources, not a total rejection of swing and earlier styles. (The first recordings of Charlie Parker and Dizzy Gillespie, in fact, contain a curious blend of older, swing, rhythmic concepts side by side with some of the most startling and complex bop melodies.) By the late 1950s, however, a point of instability had been reached once again. Mainstream jazz had arrived at a complacent plateau in its development and only some sweeping changes could jar it loose.

Signs of the impending revolution had been in evidence for some time. In the late 1950s Miles Davis, who had always been in the vanguard of jazz developments, was experimenting once again, this time with "modal scales" in place of the traditional major/minor harmonic system and its corresponding chord progressions. The fruits of Davis's labors are evident as early as 1958 in the Columbia recording *Milestones* (CS 9428) and especially in the 1959 recording

Kind of Blue (CS 8163). The Davis composition "Milestones" (labeled "Miles" on the record) consists of a simple staccato melody over a sequence of alternating Dorian and Aeolian scales. There are no moving sequences of chord changes and the improvisation is based solely on the modal scales. Davis's shift away from chord progressions—which by the late 1950s had become extremely complex and fast moving—reflected his desire for simpler harmonic backgrounds and a freer approach to melodic improvisation. He also challenged, for the first time in jazz history, the role of functional harmony as a mainstay of the jazz composition and performance. But tampering with traditional, functional harmony was only the first of many changes that were to take place in the new jazz. By the mid-1960s, virtually every element of the music had been affected: the rhythm, melody, texture, tone color, and especially the form.

Ornette Coleman and the Avant-Garde

Changes this sweeping could not happen suddenly, and there were many extramusical factors that influenced the new direction in jazz. Chief among these was a growing awareness of Black Nationalism among some black musicians and their black audiences. That this new movement would have gained momentum during the late 1950s and early 1960s is not particularly surprising following the Civil Rights legislation, the Montgomery Bus Boycott, and the emergence of the outspoken black leaders Dr. Martin Luther King, Jr., and Malcolm X. The frequent protest marches, demonstrations, and "sit-ins" in the South created a new unity among the black populace. When the new equality came about more slowly than expected, the subsequent discontent made itself manifest in a variety of ways, among them a new and revolutionary black music.[1] The new jazz did not merely enlarge or expand the musical resources of the past, it rejected them totally. Although many performers eventually involved themselves in this new movement, later known as the avant-garde, a young alto saxophonist led the way with some early recordings that literally fractured the traditional foundations of jazz itself. His name is Ornette Coleman.

Coleman is a native of Fort Worth, Texas, and a product of the rhythm-and-blues tradition in the Southwest. A self-taught performer, he moved to Los Angeles in 1954, worked at a variety of odd jobs, and studied music theory and composition. While in California, Coleman recognized that jazz was showing signs of stagnation; there were the predictable chord sequences and melodic and rhythmic patterns, and the music was losing much of its spontaneous improvisatory character. Jazz groups functioned more as a collection of individual soloists, and the collective group spirit that had been part of jazz from the beginning was lost. Coleman espoused a "free group improvisation"—one without preconceived rules, tunes, or structures in which the individuals were free to improvise collectively. As Coleman soon learned, however, totally free, collective improvisation was difficult to accomplish and it was not until 1960, with his recording *Free Jazz* (Atlantic SD 1364), that it was realized completely. Here two separate quartets improvise simultaneously, without the benefit of a rehearsal or any preparation whatsoever. By contrast, Coleman's earlier recordings (*The Shape of Jazz to Come* [Atlantic S-1317], *Change of the Century* [Atlantic S-1327], *This Is Our Music* [Atlantic S-1353], etc.), as daring as they were, all contain evidence of structure or order. Coleman composed most of the selections, and they all have some semblance of organization, regardless how vague.

Although he began his experiments in California, the controversy surrounding Ornette Coleman did not reach a peak until his debut in New York's Five Spot Café in the fall of 1959. During the three years that followed, Coleman made a total of seven recordings for Atlantic Records, recordings that sparked perhaps the most intense debate ever in the history of jazz. Not only was he and his pianoless quartet a controversial subject among jazz fans and critics, but the musicians themselves were confused and divided on the merits of his music. Cries of "antijazz" and "charlatanism" were common and in some cases justified. (Coleman's music did represent, in many ways, a negation of traditional principles governing jazz performance.) In his attempt to be free from structural, harmonic, and melodic formulae, his music often took on a disorganized and sometimes nearly chaotic appearance. Beginnings and endings were uncertain, and the steady pulse of the rhythm section, characteristic of nearly all jazz, was often abandoned for a freer shifting or changing pulse—or perhaps no pulse at all. To add insult to injury, Coleman performed on a plastic alto saxophone during the early years ("I bought it originally because I needed a new horn badly, and I felt I could not afford a new brass instrument") and this unusual instrument gave his playing a strident, almost nasal sound.

Coleman's best-known recording from his early period is his composition "Lonely Woman" (Atlantic S-1317). This performance typifies in many ways his new free jazz in practice. Although far from being totally free—there is a recognizable theme played in quasi-unison by Coleman and trumpeter Don Cherry along with a steady, although at times loosely related, rhythmic foundation—this performance is certainly a departure from postbop recordings of the late 1950s. The precision unison beginnings and endings are notably absent and Coleman's wailing, blues-oriented choruses tested even the most liberal of ears. "Lonely Woman," of course, has become a classic of the early avant-garde and in retrospect seems closer to the bebop of the late 1950s than the free jazz experiments that were to follow.

Ornette Coleman retired from performing in late 1962 after an appearance at Town Hall, and for the next two years concentrated his efforts on learning the trumpet and violin. In the meantime, the new jazz which he so boldly helped shape entered a phase of even more extreme development in the hands of John Coltrane and his disciples Eric Dolphy, Pharoah Sanders, Archie Shepp, and Albert Ayler.

John Coltrane

Early career

As a musical revolutionary, John Coltrane was a very palatable figure. Unlike Ornette Coleman, who had never apprenticed in a conventional jazz band, Coltrane was a veteran of many jazz groups including Dizzy Gillespie's big band and the influential Miles Davis Quintet. His credentials were solid. He had proved himself as an outstanding soloist time and time again, and his remarkable technique and facility became at first the envy and later the model of scores of saxophonists throughout the 1960s and 1970s. At a time when Rollins was perfecting his "thematic improvisation" technique, Coltrane was playing with a demonic intensity and romantic fervor unrivaled in the jazz world.

As a member of the Miles Davis Quintet in the late 1950s, Coltrane pioneered the new, animated, quasi-bop solo that made use of modal scales. The Dorian was his favorite and in his hands the solo line became a blur of rapidly moving scale passages, twisting, turning—seemingly defying all the rules of the underlying rhythmic accompaniment. This so-called "sheets of sound" technique was more than just a virtuoso demonstration, it was also a rejection of the carefully controlled postbop solo—a turning away from the older ideals of proportion, balance, tension, and repose. This helps explain the lack of variety and contrast in much of Coltrane's playing from this period; for all of its excitement, the range of contrast and expression is actually very limited. A case in point can be seen even in Coltrane's relatively conservative "Giant Steps," recorded in 1959. Viewed by many as perhaps his best recorded improvisation on chord changes, this performance is a blazing display of unrelenting virtuosity. Hardly a beat is left silent, and the intensity that pervades the performance is continuous from beginning to end. The long-standing principles of tension and repose that had served for so many jazz players in the past were clearly abandoned.

Indian and African Influences

When John Coltrane turned and embraced the avant-garde in 1961, he did so as a full-fledged musical revolutionary seeking musical inspiration from non-Western cultures, specifically India and Africa. African music had not played a major role in jazz since its beginnings, and even then the connection, although essential, was rather remote—mostly in the area of rhythm and specifically swing. But in the 1960s, the mysticism and exoticism of African music provided the black jazz musician with a new inspirational resource, a clear alternative to the Western musical conventions and ideals that had dominated jazz since its start.

For the jazz player, the principal novelty of African music lay in its wealth of instrumental colors. Various kinds of flutes, reed, and percussion instruments, including the thumb piano, rattles, bells, and conga drums found increasing usage throughout the 1960s. Some groups used multiple drummers to imitate the polymetric effects heard in the African percussion ensemble (Coltrane's *Meditations*, Impulse AS-9110). Reed players (Coltrane, Rollins, and Shepp included) began exploring a new concept of tone quality, one that employed various shrieks and growls—supposedly in imitation of primitive African musical sounds.

Indian music possessed an exoticism similar to African music and had the additional advantage of an underlying philosophical system that was decidedly non-Western and therefore a great attraction to the Black Nationalist jazz musicians. The chief catalyst for interest in Indian music in the United States was the sitarist Ravi Shankar, who arrived in the early 1960s as a visiting professor at UCLA. Shankar attracted the attention of some influential jazz musicians, who found in his music new instrumental colors, timbres, and textures. (Coltrane and Eric Dolphy actually expressed a desire to travel to India and study with the master when he returned.)

The fact that both Indian music and African music were the products of "Third World" countries proved even a greater inspiration for the avant-garde jazz musician. Whereas Ornette Coleman's motives were primarily musical—a search for greater freedom from established rules and conventions, Coltrane and his disciples sought a counter-European solution: the union of jazz and the music of nonwhite cultures. The products of Coltrane's efforts culminated in two albums: *A Love Supreme* (Impulse 77) and *Ascension* (Impulse A-95). These were among the more controversial jazz recordings of the 1960s and helped establish John Coltrane, perhaps more than Ornette Coleman, as the new visionary leader of the avant-garde. Frustrated by mounting criticism at home, Ornette Coleman enjoyed a successful tour of Europe in 1965, appearing at the Berlin Jazz Festival; but during the same year John Coltrane was named to the Downbeat Hall of Fame and Jazzman of the Year, and his *A Love Supreme* was voted Record of the Year, Best Jazz Composition, and Jazz Album of the Year.

Mainstream Jazz

The impact of the avant-garde movement did not stifle once and for all the more traditional forms of jazz. Mainstream jazz continued, but its dependence on functional harmony, pop tunes, blues models, and a steady pulse began to wane. In addition, the introduction of Afro/Asian strains broadened the complexion of jazz to such an extent that the way was opened for other musical intrusions, notably the bossa nova and rock.

Bossa Nova

The bossa nova developed in Brazil during the late 1950s and was an outgrowth of the older samba, a dance of Afro-Brazilian origins. Its two characteristic musical features are a free-floating syncopated rhythm and a multiplicity of tonal centers, traits that made it attractive to American jazzmen. The rhythmic peculiarities of the bossa nova were completely compatible with jazz swing and phrasing and gave rise to the jazz bossa—a hybrid jazz form and one that had great commercial potential as a new kind of dance music. Although the creators were Brazilians (Antonio Carlos Jobim and Luiz Bonfá), many American jazzmen participated in its initial development in this country; included among them are Stan Getz, Charlie Byrd, and Jim Hall. During the 1970s the bossa nova and its related styles integrated completely with American jazz and still account for a substantial proportion of Latin-influenced jazz tunes performed today.

Rock

The mixture of rock and jazz was a much more gradual development. Originally thought to be incompatible with jazz because of its endless repetition, simple harmonic schemes, and the monotonous regularity of "on the beat accents," rock did not fuse with jazz until the late 1960s—several years after it was brought to the United States by British vocal groups. The first successful commercial jazz/rock recordings were made by the popular groups Blood, Sweat and Tears and Chicago Transit Authority. Their success pointed the way for bolder experiments by older, established jazz players like Miles Davis (*In a Silent Way* [Columbia CS 9875] and *Bitches Brew* [Columbia GP 26], both recorded in 1969). Rock brought to jazz an increased volume level and a greater use of amplified instruments, particularly the electric guitar, bass, and keyboards (pianos and synthesizers), Attempts to find ways of varying the repetitious rhythmic, harmonic, and melodic patterns of rock led jazz musicians to new levels of virtuosity, levels not experienced since the end of the bebop era. The drums, for example, were released from the duties of mere accompaniment and assumed a role as an equal solo instrument. (In many recordings, the drums appear to be continuously soloing behind the other instruments.)

The net result of the new exotic influences was a multiplicity of styles unprecedented in jazz history. Never before had so many different variations coexisted under one heading. Jazz was not one kind of music any longer, but an eclectic amalgam of styles, and the orderly evolution process which had shaped jazz from its earliest days had ended. But there were positive benefits also. Jazz gained a much broader audience during this period, not the intimate audience of the small night club—the traditional forum for hearing jazz in years past (jazz night clubs, in fact, suffered a noticeable decline during the 1960s)—but a larger and more heterogenous audience. Taking a cue from the large rock festivals so popular during the 1960s, jazz moved to the concert stage and to open-air festivals and in doing so set the tone for the next phase in the music's development: the pop-jazz of the 1970s.

8

Sonny Rollins
and the Avant-Garde

1961: The First Sabbatical Ends

Sonny Rollins ended his first retirement in the fall of 1961. The two years that he spent away from performing music had clearly changed his perspective. During this time he composed, practiced, exercised, and generally attempted to renew himself both physically and mentally. The music business in the late 1950s had been an exhausting experience for the jazz musician: alcohol, drugs, the rigors of night-club performances. Rollins needed an opportunity for contemplative reflection and he found it. But jazz had changed during his absence, and upon his return Rollins soon found himself in a much different musical environment. Gone were the faithful jazz audiences who had followed the progress of bebop through the postbop and funk stages. There was a new "awareness," a new standard for the black jazz musician—one that did not necessarily take into consideration the accomplishments of the players of the recent past; one, in fact, that rebelled against them. No performer, not even Rollins in his reclusive existence of these two years, was unaware of the controversy generated by the new music, the avant-garde. Ornette Coleman's Five Spot Café appearances and his recordings for Atlantic records were much publicized and the resulting criticism divided musicians and listeners alike. And then there was John Coltrane. He had matured as an artist and was beginning to cast his lot with the avant-garde. His departure from mainstream jazz and his turn toward Afro/Asian musical influences guaranteed him a secure place in the new revolutionary music.

Rollins's position, on the other hand, was particularly perplexing. Acceptance in the avant-garde called for a rejection of the objectives of postbop performance: the very technique that he helped perfect. He might have resisted, as many jazzmen do when styles change (Louis Armstrong, Lester Young, and Coleman Hawkins all maintained their original orientation in spite of evolutionary changes in style), but Rollins preferred to be regarded as part of the new generation of jazz performers, not the old; rather than the venerated position of veteran performer, he sought to participate in the new revolutionary music and wanted a chance to express himself in the new music's terms.

Rollins approached this challenge cautiously: upon renewing his performing career in 1961, he assembled a new quartet consisting of Jim Hall, guitar, Bob Cranshaw, bass, and Ben Riley or H. T. Saunders, drums. Jim Hall was the best-known performer of the sidemen: he had recorded widely with many of the leading exponents of West Coast ("Cool") jazz including Chico Hamilton, Jimmy Giuffre, and Lee Konitz. After some time concertizing, and much time rehearsing, the quartet recorded *The Bridge* during January and February of 1962.

For many jazz aficionados, particularly those nurtured in the avant-garde of the 1960s, Sonny Rollins's career begins with this LP for RCA. Because of his two-year silence, many are unaware of his earlier recordings and regard *The Bridge* as the beginning of a career rather than the continuation of one after a long absence. This is at least partially due to the many publicized accounts of Rollins's practice habits on the Williamsburg Bridge during his two-year hiatus. But Rollins had, after all, genuine reasons for seeking solace during those lonely practice sessions on the bridge. There, on the pedestrian walkway, he could concentrate, free from the anxiety of disturbing his neighbors and removed from the pressures of urban living.

The musical content of the album suggests that the title may have a dual significance. On the one hand it documents an important experience in Rollins's life, his lonely vigil in an attempt to renew himself. But on the other, some selections are truly a "bridge" between the Rollins on the 1950s and the renewed master who is about to embrace the avant-garde. These extremes are sharply differentiated in the music.

Of the six selections, four of them ("Without a Song," "Where Are You?," "God Bless the Child," "You Do Something to Me") are reminiscent of the Rollins of the 1950s. They are standard tunes and are performed in a conventional manner—recognizable, paraphrased melodies and "boppish" style choruses on the fast tunes; lyrical, nostalgic interpretations on the ballads. The rendition of the standard "Where Are You?" is a classic Rollins performance of a familiar ballad: the unhurried paraphrase of the tune's theme, complete with many alterations of phrasing and rhythmic delays and surprises. But unlike his ballads of the 1950s ("Body and Soul," "How are Things in Glocca Morra,?" etc.) he does not improvise thematically, but stays very close to the theme and ends very simply—no cadenza and on the tonic note (Eb).

Both "Without a Song" and "You Do Something to Me" sound deceptively like the Rollins of the late 1950s, especially when he paraphrases the melodies. His improvised choruses, however, contain mixtures of thematic improvisation along with nonmelodic, abstract figuration—a juxtaposition that would not have occurred in Rollins's playing before his retirement. The two most striking selections on this record are the Rollins originals "The Bridge" and "John S." Here Rollins makes his first recorded attempts at a freer style of playing. "John S.," in particular, is a Coleman-like composition featuring a disjunctive introduction and coda that appear to have no connection with the improvised sections of the tune. Rollins's choruses mix staccato figures on one note with some halting bop figures and a rhythmic line that often appears dislodged from the rhythm section's beat. These are bold experiments for Rollins and there is nothing in the other tunes of the album to suggest that Rollins was inclined toward the avant-garde. So different are "John S." and "The Bridge" from "Where Are You?" and "You Do Something to Me," for example, that it is hard to believe that they were recorded by the same person at the same session.

The choice of personnel for Rollins's quartet is also puzzling. With material like "John S." and "The Bridge," why include a guitarist such as Jim Hall? A competent, lyrical, melodic soloist, his understated playing does not seem compatible with the two Rollins originals. And since the group played together both before and after the recording was made, presumably this incongruity had existed for some time. The answer lies, perhaps, in the unique position that Rollins occupied in the history of post-World War II jazz. Rollins, perhaps, was uncertain as to what stance to take upon returning to active performance; his ambiguous feelings about his position as a leading figure

in the 1950s and desire to play a role in the new music may have led
him to compromise by structuring a group that allowed him to do
both. In any event, Rollins's uncertainty was only temporary. Within
six months after the sessions for *The Bridge* had ended, Rollins
recorded two additional albums for RCA, recordings that document
his completely changed attitude concerning jazz improvisation. For
the next few years, at least, Rollins ceases to be a melodic player and
joins the avant-garde.

The Free Jazz Years

Sonny Rollins's style of improvising was forever altered by the success of his early free jazz experiments beginning with *The Bridge.*
Throughout the 1960s, whether the material was of the "standard"
variety or a jazz original, his playing continued to reflect his new
avant-garde stance. Only for a brief period toward the end of his
association with RCA in 1965 (see discussion ahead) did he revert to a
more conventional postbop instrumentation and format. At other
times, his commitment as a free jazz performer was total and
unswerving.

What's New?

Rollins's second album for RCA is the product of several separate
recording sessions and some seemingly incongruent juxtapositions
of personnels and styles. The first four selections have essentially the
same personnel as *The Bridge* (the only change being the addition of
percussion). But the remainder of side two has Rollins together with
two of Ornette Coleman's former sidemen: drummer Billy Higgins
and trumpeter Don Cherry. The material is similarly divided, with
four Sonny Rollins originals for the former group ("Don't Stop the
Carnival," "Jungoso," "Bluesongo," and "Brownskin Girl") and three
standard tunes ("You Are My Lucky Star," "I Could Write a Book," and
"There Will Never Be Another You") performed in a free style by the
latter. (Those expecting to hear the Bob Haggart—Johnny Burke
classic ballad "What's New?" will be disappointed to learn that the
album title has nothing to do with this frequently recorded jazz
ballad.)

The liner notes loudly proclaim *What's New?* as a bossa-nova
recording, but any resemblance to this popular Brazilian import is
very remote. A good case could be made for "calypso," however. Both

"Brownskin Girl" and "Don't Stop the Carnival" have a chorus and "call and response" pattern reminiscent of the Harry Belafonte calypso recordings popular in the mid-1950s; even the rhythmic figure ♩.♪♩♪ is the same.

Rollins reveals a new side to his playing with the two originals "Jungoso" and "Bluesongo." "Jungoso" is a themeless improvisation constructed over the static base figure ¢♩.♪♩♩.♪♩♩, that uses the Bb Dorian mode and Bb pentatonic scale almost exclusively. The modes and the pentatonic scales derived from them were in fairly common usage by the early 1960s, although it was rare to find them presented in such a clear and unaltered fashion (see example 44).

Example 44. "Jungoso"

Sonny's tone has also changed from the hard but clear, throaty sound of the 1950s (probably produced by using a stiff reed) to a somewhat harsher and yet muffled sound, used often in combination with harmonic double-stops and notes of indeterminate pitch. The alterations in tone, sound, and lack of precision were traits shared by many avant-garde performers and resulted from their rejection of European musical ideals.

"Bluesongo," the other Rollins original, is a trio for tenor, bass, and bongos—an unusual instrumentation that contains very little harmonic definition. This is probably exactly what Rollins had in mind, because although the tune is structured as a blues piece in C-minor, there is so much "outside" playing that the feeling for the key is sometimes lost. The melody and Rollins's improvised choruses are organized around a simple, pentatonic motive (see example 45) which undergoes much repetition during the course of the performance. The harmonic ambiguity is further increased by emphasizing the notes D and Ab, thereby creating a feeling of bitonality reminiscent of Rollins's earlier "Blue Seven."

Example 45. "Bluesongo"

As unorthodox as these selections are, they are still rather conservative pieces that illustrate Rollins's newly discovered manner of communicating with the audience through simplicity and repetition. The real adventure on this recording comes with his free treatment of the standards "You Are My Lucky Star," "I Could Write a Book," and "There Will Never Be Another You." Only in the last selection is there any attempt to refer to the melody of the original, the others being free adaptations that use the general outline and structure of the tune as a guide. "You Are My Lucky Star," in particular, has an abstract, staccato beginning played by the tenor and trumpet; only when Rollins plays the alternating eight measures alone with the rhythm section is there any recognizable hint of a theme. The connection with the original tune in "I Could Write a Book' is also vague; both Cherry and Rollins play completely "outside" choruses, harmonically removed from the chord progressions of the original tune. This was possible, and for avant-gardists desirable, when no chordal instrument (piano, guitar, etc.) was present to keep the harmony in check. Rollins, of course, was always known for his harmonic "strayings" (see chapter 5), but these were usually of short duration and not as extreme.

Our Man in Jazz

Jazz performers have always debated the merits of live recordings versus those completed in the recording studio. The studio had the advantage of a controlled environment that allowed corrections or improvements as needed. The night club, on the other hand, was usually a less predictable setting, but it offered the immediate response and encouragement of the audience and, as Rollins observed, in the event of a bad start "it gives the performer the chance to redeem himself sometime during the course of the evening." For Sonny Rollins, the choice was clear: he much preferred performances recorded in front of live audiences, and the first free jazz performance recorded in this manner appears on record as *Our Man in Jazz* (RCA LPM-2612).

Seen in perspective, the two earlier albums for RCA were mere preparations for this one—his first all-out effort in free, collective improvisation. Recorded at the Village Gate in New York's Greenwich Village, it is probably Rollins's best recorded venture in the avant-garde. Sonny calls it "my first conscious, deliberate attempt to do something in a free jazz vein," and free it is. The entire album consists of only three tunes (lengthy, wrung-out performances were in vogue with the avant-garde: "Oleo," "Doxy," and "Dearly Beloved"—two Rollins originals and a standard. Both "Doxy" and "Dearly Beloved" contain moments of inspired, as well as abstract, nonmelodic playing from Rollins and Cherry, but the real strength of these performances comes from the free rhythmic feeling created by bassist Bob Cranshaw and drummer Billy Higgins. This unique rhythmic feeling is one of the most important and enduring contributions of free jazz and also one aspect of the music that is often overlooked. With the lack of melodic or harmonic limits, the rhythmic accompaniment of free jazz becomes an important means of generating the continuity needed for the performance. It contributes a lively sense of swing that frees the improviser from the rhythmic and melodic clichés of previous eras. Drummers Billy Higgins and Ed Blackwell were the originators of this style of drumming, and, as former sidemen with Ornette Coleman, both played a major role in the initial success of his free jazz experiments.

"Oleo" is Rollins's free jazz tour de force. Its abstract, breakneck beginning and ending, interrupted with a slow, blueslike section near the end, makes this tune the most convincing of Rollins's avant-garde excursions. Like all good free jazz performers, he avoids clear statements of the original melody, preferring staggered statements of it instead, but there is enough constructive playing present to give the tune a feeling of logical development. *Our Man in Jazz* may also represent Rollins's and Cherry's best effort at collective improvisation, the most cherished and yet difficult aspect of the performance in which to succeed. Collective improvisation, in the free jazz context, is really improvisation by association; lacking any preconceived plan, the players merely suggest ideas to each other and then take turns in developing them. Rollins makes most of the "suggestions" (perhaps a motive or a familiar quotation), which are then usually echoed by Cherry and the rhythm section. This procedure works only when the players are linked together by a certain sympathetic bond—a thorough familiarity with jazz phraseology and rhythmic nuance that enables them to develop material spontaneously and melodically.

Unfortunately, collective, totally free improvisation was a risky business that more often than not failed. For a group to improvise collectively without the aid of any preparation whatsoever required a level of communication among members that was difficult to sustain for lengthy periods of time. Coleman, Coltrane, and Rollins were occasionally successful in these attempts, but there were many more failures, and most free jazz performers, including Rollins, eventually lost interest in the procedure.

Sonny Meets Hawk

Encouraged by the reception given *Our Man in Jazz*, Rollins continued to develop his brand of free jazz throughout the remainder of 1962 and 1963. In July 1963 he appeared at the Newport Jazz Festival, playing opposite his idol and mentor Coleman Hawkins, and a week later the two met in RCA's Studio B in New York to record *Sonny Meets Hawk* (LPM 2712), Sonny's fifth album for that label.

Rollins sets the tone almost immediately on "Yesterdays" by playing an unusual chorus, made up largely of trills, and Hawkins follows suit with a disjunctive, although comparatively more melodic, chorus of his own. For the remainder of the recording, made up mostly of first takes, both players seem to be pushing the limits of free jazz improvisation as far as they can, although Rollins's use of overtones ("Lover Man"), trills, and off-pitch playing is the more excessive. (In both "At McKies'" and "All the Things You Are," Sonny's playing ventures so far from the implicit harmonic foundation, that it approaches a near atonal level—especially in the latter tune, where he plays a countertheme to Hawkins's paraphrase of the melody.)

Why two of the greatest melodic improvisers should have teamed up to play what is essentially "nonmelodic" jazz is a puzzle at best; furthermore, the incongruity is made all the more striking by the presence of the conventional rhythm section of piano, bass, and drums. Ornette Coleman, and later Rollins himself, proved that collective improvisation in the free style could work, but that it works best when all the players are equally free. *Sonny Meets Hawk* sounds closer to Sonny's earlier efforts *The Bridge* and *What's New?*, where a disparity exists between the conventional, straight-ahead rhythm section and Sonny's harmonically free (almost atonal) improvising.

The avant-garde in decline

For all the excitement it caused and the changes it brought about, free jazz, in its most extreme form, was a relatively shortlived movement, and Rollins knew it. As a resourceful musician, he was able to draw from it what he needed: it did help liberate his thinking both melodically, rhythmically, and harmonically, and it gave him a spectacular start after his two-year absence.

But jazz audiences tired quickly of this brash new music that was devoid of recognizable themes or melodic development and their initial curiosity eventually turned to indifference as the movement wore on. (Rollins's twenty-five-minute performance of "Oleo" at the Village Gate in 1962 [*Our Man in Jazz*], for example, drew only polite applause and the audience became audibly restless during the performance of "Doxy" that same evening.)

In the end, free jazz was a novel idea, but one whose strict application could not work. It had to be tempered, and virtually all of those who tried to play it found ways to adapt it to their particular performance situations. Rollins adopted most of the mannerisms of the music—the increased intensity, volume, repertoire of new sounds (growls, shrieks, overtones, etc.)—but unlike John Coltrane and his followers he avoided the more exotic influences of African and Asian music. His melodic lines were as nonmelodic as most, thus reinforcing Albert Ayler's claim: "It's not about notes any more—it's about feelings." The majority of his recorded performances, at least, gave structural continuity a low priority, thus the beginnings and endings of tunes were often totally improvised, with many anticlimactic starts and stops—all in keeping with the unpredictable nature of an avant-garde performance.

Critics and educated listeners might have been more outspoken in their opposition to the excesses of free jazz except for the fact that they too were often confused. Many feared making premature judgments before a more complete perspective of the music could be gained—a mistake that haunted some who too quickly criticized the relatively conservative bebop movement, the only other revolution in jazz history.

Those who were bold enough to dismiss free jazz as nonsense usually missed the point anyway. Free jazz, like the corresponding avant-garde movement in European art music (which was much more experimental), is really beyond criticism in the usual musical sense. It is catalytic music and can be appreciated for the changes that it provoked, but not as an end in itself, for there was no way to evaluate it with existing criteria. If a player's quest for freedom in playing leads him toward nonmelodic, arhythmic, structure-free music, then the established methods used in judging a conventional performance cannot be employed.

Sonny Rollins's music from this period also defies evaluation. For him, free collective improvisation was merely one phase of his musical development—a bold and daring phase, but one he would soon temper as he returned once again to a more moderate style of playing.

More experimentation in the Late 1960s

Sonny's departure from free jazz during the mid-1960s corresponds roughly with the beginning of his association with Impulse Records. As is the case with most recording artists, a new contract often means new ideas and new directions. With totally free jazz in a state of decline, Sonny needed some new directions by 1965. But his change was not as dramatic as critics and reviewers at first thought.[1] True, he did record mostly standard tunes during this time (*There Will Never Be Another You* [IA-9349] and *On Impulse* [A-91] are composed mostly of standards) and he did on occasion even play a recognizable version of the melody at the beginning and end of tunes. But, even in the wildest free jazz days, standards have always constituted a significant part of his repertoire ("I play them because people know them and can tell if you're doing them right or not"), even if they were treated so freely as to be barely recognizable. So Sonny's real adjustment during this period had not so much to do with his own playing—it continued to be as unpredictable as it was in the early 1960s—but with a change in the personnel and instrumentation of his group.

New instrumentation

After reflecting on the future of free jazz and the avant-garde movement in general, Rollins decided once again on a conventional rhythm-section instrumentation of piano, bass, and drums. It had been nearly two years since he had used a piano on a recording (Paul Bley on *Sonny Meets Hawk* was the last), and before that not since 1959, the year of his first extended retirement.

The avant-gardists viewed the presence of the piano as a restriction that curbed their free improvising. As the principal chordal instrument of the rhythm section, its purpose was to define the harmonic framework of the tune. But in so doing, it also restricted the

harmonic freedom of the soloist. After some early experiments (Ornette Coleman used a pianist on his first recording, *Something Else*
[Contemporary C3551], most avant-gardists worked without one.

Rollins, at different times, used two pianists for his mid-1960s
recordings: Ray Bryant, who performed with him during his days
with the Max Roach Quintet, and Tommy Flannagan, former member
of the Miles Davis Quintet and many other groups from the 1950s.
Both were established performers of the postbop school and neither
had experimented with free jazz.

The presence of the pianist, and the more conservative rhythm
section, especially on *There Will Never Be Another You*, served to
restore a sense of order and balance that was missing from many of
Sonny's recordings of previous years. Everyone played with more
moderation and maintained an almost bebop format of paraphrased
melodies in the beginning, and an orderly procession of solo
choruses. Sonny's playing was the only exception; it varied considerably from tune to tune and even within the same tune.

Continues nonmelodic style

Occasionally he played long, abstract, boplike solos ("Three Little
Words" [IA-9349]) reminiscent of the preretirement days, but the
majority of the time his choruses took on a peculiar atonal, or
nonmelodic character. After an unusually free interpretation of the
melody of "On Green Dolphin Street" (IA-9349) and an equally free
first chorus, for example, he softly sustains a single note (Bb), refer-
ring to it from time to time through the piano chorus and after.
References to the tune's theme are also frequent in many of his
improvisations—especially at the beginning of each eight-measure
period ("Blue Room" from *On Impulse*). During one of the choruses in
"There Will Never Be Another You," Sonny even plays the melody
intact—a rare gesture for any improvising jazz musician. Another
improvisation consists of repeated statements of the melody only
("To a Wild Rose" from *There Will Never Be Another You*).

This need to be unorthodox or free applied more to endings,
perhaps, than to any other part of the tune. Many never seem to end
at all but merely trail off (or fade) after a number of false starts and
stops. Some contain quotation of familiar tunes ("The Continental" in
There Will Never Be Another You) and others have anticlimactic
cadenzas, some of which are quite extended. (These are often the
most spontaneous, although disorganized, segments of a typical

Rollins performance during this time.) Still others are strung together like medleys ("There Will Never Be Another You" and "Three Little Words"), with little or no stop in between.

The late 1960s

In pursuing an unorthodox manner of playing, Rollins's music reflects the confusion experienced by many other jazzmen of this time. The post-avant-garde period found jazz in perhaps the greatest slump in its fifty years of recorded history. It was a period of relative inactivity, especially for those recovering from the shock of free jazz, rock, and the subsequent loss of jazz audiences.

Sonny Rollins was also affected. He worked only intermittently during this period and recorded very little. Between 1966 and 1969, in fact, he made only two LPs, and they seemed once again to reaffirm his commitment to experimentation and nonconformity.

Alfie (Impulse AS-9111) contains "Alfie's Theme" (not to be confused with Burt Bacharach's popular title tune "Alfie"), composed for the film score a year earlier, along with five other jazz originals. All of the free jazz devices are present on this recording: the nonmelodic or quasi-melodic soloing, the repetition of themes, impromptu endings, and the regular symmetrical phrasing. Only two months elapsed before Impulse released his next album, and very little, if any, change took place in his concept of improvising. In *East Broadway Run Down* (Impulse S-9121), issued in 1967, Sonny continues the free approach of *Alfie* and the other recordings of the mid-1960s, with one important exception: Included between two uninhibited free jazz originals is the Richard Rodgers standard "We Kiss in a Shadow," performed in a conventional manner. Here he proves his loyalty to standards and an ability to recapture his style of the 1950s. But *East Broadway Run Down* was the last of its kind; he would embark on his second extended sabbatical in the fall of 1969, and when he returned nearly two years later the experimentation of the 1960s ended and a new era of pop/jazz had already begun.

9

The Recordings of the 1970s

The Jazz/Rock Fusion

The year 1969 will go down as a momentous year in the history of jazz, for during that year Miles Davis completed two remarkable LPs for Columbia records: *In a Silent Way* and *Bitches Brew*. These truly unique and forward-looking recordings marked the first attempt at a jazz/rock union by a major jazz performer—an amalgamation that would completely alter the course of jazz for many years to come.

Why it worked

The jazz/rock fusion, as it eventually became known, arrived at a particularly propitious time in jazz history: the free jazz movement had cast jazz as an esoteric brand of experimental music that in the end failed to communicate successfully with the public at large. It had been a self-indulgent exercise of music for musicians' sake, and the net effects were felt in the loss of audience support, record sales, and interest among the established record companies. By the time Miles Davis's recordings arrived on the market, many jazz musicians were desperate for a merger with another, and especially more popular, form of music.

As a potential partner, rock was the perfect candidate for the mix. It offered many new colors and melodic and especially rhythmic concepts that were novel to jazz; and as music it already had a proven record of success in exciting the public. Young audiences, by the late 1960s, had been thoroughly weaned on its increased volume level and repetitious rhythm and guitar-oriented instrumentation, and they especially cherished its role as a leading expression of rebellion against the establishment. But like most popular music, pure rock was simple to a fault and many young fans yearned for more challenging listening experiences.

The earliest efforts

In 1968, the groups Blood, Sweat and Tears and Chicago provided the answer. Composed of some former, but relatively unknown, jazz musicians, they first succeeded in altering the traditional rock instrumentation and format through the introduction of intricate brass parts and some surprising jazz solos. Jazz musicians were quick to follow their lead, and within two years of Miles Davis's pioneering recordings, the first fusion group, Weather Report, began to record. Staffed by two of Miles's former sidemen, Josef Zawinul and Wayne Shorter, theirs became the first of the new groups to fuse electrified rock and jazz in the new high-decibel format. Weather Report was soon followed by two other groups: Chick Corea's Return to Forever and Herbie Hancock's Head Hunters. Both leaders were former sidemen with Miles Davis, and both were participants in his pioneering recordings of 1969.

More fusions

The jazz/rock fusion bands of the early 1970s were true jazz bands in every sense of the word. There was a high level of skilled improvisation in what they produced and a sense of creativity that accompanied their bold explorations. But the spectacular success of these groups inspired scores of performers of every musical persuasion and background, many of whom attempted compromising fusions of their own. Soon the jazz/rock fusion became the jazz/rock/soul/ pop/funk fusion and the eclecticism continued and increased throughout the 1970s. Jazz, of course, has always been fusion music. Throughout its history, it survived numerous "fusions" with European art music, Afro-Cuban music, Latin-American music, bossa nova, and others. But not until the 1970s were there so many fusions taking place simultaneously, and never before had they been of such a popular magnitude. So diverse are the categories today, in fact, that there are potentially, at least, as many styles of jazz as there are performers to create them. Sonny Rollins is one of these performers, who, after a distinguished career as a melodic improviser and later as a free jazz player, created his own style for the 1970s. But in formulating his style for that decade, he completely departed from the ranks of the other major fusion players.

Sonny's Return

The fusion idea was nothing new to Sonny Rollins. His entire improvisatory style had been a fusion of sorts: a continuous juxtaposition of seemingly incongruent elements of every type and dimension. On the lowest level there were the unusual harmonic and rhythmic eccentricities, and the surprising quotations of foreign melodic material mixed with some of the most inspired demonstrations of melodic improvisation. From a broader viewpoint, he was constantly exploring the combination of jazz and unlikely music types such as the calypso, cowboy, and vaudeville tunes. He had even experimented with unusual meters and had been one of the participants in the first all-waltz-time jazz recording (*Max Roach Plus Four: Jazz in 3/4 Time*). And in between there were the peculiar tunes that didn't seem proper jazz material ("There's No Business Like Show Business," "I Know That You Know," and "Rock-A-Bye Your Baby with a Dixie Melody") but were transformed anyway into brilliant examples of spontaneous improvisation. So Sonny had always experimented, and had always been an imaginative jazz player.

The events that shaped the fusion of the 1970s, however, were different from those that motivated his unorthodoxy of the postbop era. Sonny's earlier experiments were an outgrowth of a natural curiosity and compulsive need to synthesize his vast wealth of musical experiences. The fusion of the early 1970s, on the other hand, offered many jazz musicians the opportunity of larger audiences and more lucrative recording and concert contracts; in short, it encouraged a type of jazz that operates in the broader area of pop music.

Sonny returned from his second sabbatical in the summer of 1971 but waited until the following year to make *Sonny Rollins' Next Album* (MSP 9042) for Milestone Records—his debut with that company. There is a little bit of everything in this recording: bebop, calypso, jazz, and rock. One thing conspicuously missing, however, is any attempt at free jazz—the tunes are very conventionally performed. His two-year hiatus had apparently helped him to abandon the avant-garde in favor of a more melodically appealing brand of jazz. *Sonny Rollins' Next Album*, in fact, is his first effort in many years to be simple and direct. In this respect, it has something in common with some of the pop/jazz recordings of the early 1970s. Rollins, however, was not then, nor could he ever be, a pop jazz artist: his musical integrity and record of accomplishment prevented him from doing this. Nevertheless, there are symbols in his music of the new fusion:

the electric bass and piano on some selections, the use of Latin percussion, and Rollins's own employment of the soprano saxophone on "Poinciana." And for the first time on a Rollins recording, there is a "funky," rock-inspired rhythm accompaniment on "Playin' in the Yard"—perhaps his first conscious concession to popular taste.

Some of the older and more typical Rollins devices are present also: an unaccompanied solo beginning and ending on "The Everywhere Calypso" and "Skylark," a quotation of an extraneous tune ("It Might as Well be Spring") in "Skylark," and a "St. Thomas"-style calypso ("The Everywhere Calypso").

Three of the five selections are Rollins originals and their melodies are modestly constructed—most are based on simple repetitive patterns. There are fewer notes in the improvised choruses, and entire choruses are derived almost entirely from major or minor pentatonic scales. "Playin' in the Yard," for example, has a theme based exclusively on the G-major pentatonic (see example 46) and choruses by Rollins based on the G-minor pentatonic (G, Bb, C, D, F).[1]

Example 46. "Playin' in the Yard"

"Keep Hold of Yourself" is a blues in C-minor. In his postbop days, the blues provided the vehicle for some of Sonny's most inspired improvising ("Blue Seven," "Misterioso," "Vierd Blues"); many of his bitonal harmonic excursions were first performed in this context. But, in 1972, Rollins's blues performances are considerably more restrained and the harmonic framework is kept simple. In "Keep Hold of Yourself," for example, Sonny's melody and improvisation are based upon the C-minor pentatonic scale (C, Eb, F, G, Bb) and the blues scale (C, Eb, F, F#, G, Bb) is not used at all. The two differ by only one note, but that one note (F#), the flatted fifth, is perhaps the most characteristic note of the blues. The result is a relaxed, tension-free performance, but one that lacks the harmonic drive of his earlier blues recordings.

Pentatonic scales eventually became one of Rollins's favorite devices of the 1970s. Many of his compositions and improvisations contain frequent use of them, and their popularity with other performers made them an aural signature of the era. As structures lacking half-steps, they were ideal for playing harmonically ambiguous modal and/or fusion jazz. Rollins even employs them on conventional standards, as in "Poinciana," but here the usage is also mixed with some harmonically "outside" playing (G-natural sustained against an Ab change).

Sonny Rollins's Next Album differs from the other first album made after long absence. *The Bridge,* recorded in 1962, followed a two-year retirement, and yet he returned sounding as strong as he did before he left. But the 1969—71 sabbatical was not a musical self-improvement break. In fact, Sonny withdrew from music altogether this time, and did not practice his horn at all. The outcome for his performing career could have been disastrous—particularly if he had lost his ability to play—or refreshing—if he came back with some startling new approach. But, he did neither: other than losing interest in the experimentation of the 1960s, Sonny continued to be as eclectic as ever, as if he were now ready to review all of his past accomplishments and perhaps add some new ones as well.

The Eclectic Rollins

With the *Sonny Rollins' Next Album* of 1972, Rollins began the most steadily productive phase of his long career. Although he recorded more in the 1950s (mostly as a sideman), and as many, or more, in the 1960s, the recordings of the 1970s were all for one label (Milestone), by one producer (Orrin Keepnews), and they appeared at regular intervals—approximately one per year. There is even a certain consistency in their format: an average of seven selections per record with approximately half being Rollins originals and, with the exception of *The Way I Feel,* at least one standard. (Sonny continued to record standards even during his most experimental phases.) The remaining selections were often the contributions of sidemen: percussionist James Mtume, pianist George Duke, trumpeter Donald Byrd, bassist Stanley Clarke, or guitarist Larry Coryell. Sonny's many changes of personnel during the 1970s appear consistent with his effort to maintain an open attitude concerning his music. "I feed on other people," he once remarked, and the imprint of his sidemen can be felt on all of his recorded efforts. Sonny's imprint is evident too, of course, not only in his improvisations but also in the original compositions that he contributed.

Rollins originals

They are of every ilk: straight-ahead jazz, calypso, disco, funk, etc.—
all revealing an eclectic outlook and, at the same time, a continuous
desire for simplicity.

The more traditional, straight-ahead, or postbop tunes form a
relatively small but significant proportion of the total output. Simple,
unadorned, straight-ahead playing was not in fashion during this
time, but Rollins was one of the few active performers of an earlier
generation who helped perfect this style of playing; perhaps because
of this, he included at least one specimen in every recording. Tunes
such as "Cosmet" and "Azalea" (*Nucleus* M-9064), "Love Man" (*Horn
Culture*, M-9051), "Hear What I'm Saying" (*Easy Living*, M-9080), and
"Silver City" (*Don't Stop the Carnival*, M-55005) all have a postbop
rhythmic feeling in common, but differ in other respects: noisy
rhythm sections and obscure themes ("Love Man"); a highly syncopated melodic rhythm ("Azalea") and a modified "sheets of sound"
technique in "Hear What I'm Saying."

The calypso type is also in evidence with the originals "Little Lu"
(*Love at First Sight*, M-9098), "The Everywhere Calypso" (*Sonny
Rollins' Next Album*, MSP-9042), and "Don't Stop the Carnival" from
the album of the same name. Rollins's interest in calypso, a long
standing one, stemmed from his mother's origin (the Virgin Islands)
and his early exposure to the music in Harlem, the location in
Manhattan of a sizable West Indian population. But unlike the earlier
"St. Thomas," his calypsos of the 1970s were not improvised thematically. They remain more faithful to the simple rhythmic and melodic
framework of their West Indian models.

The real surprise in tune types comes with Rollins's introduction
of originals with the contemporary "disco" beat. Most jazz musicians
found this dance type particularly abhorrent when first introduced
because of the incessant pounding of the bass drum $^c\!\sqcup\!\sqcup\!\sqcup$.
Rollins, however, defended the compatibility of dance music and jazz
("There's nothing wrong with it," he once remarked), and he re-
minded his critics that his appearances with Miles Davis, John Coltrane, and others at the Audubon Ballroom in the 1950s were billed as
"dances," and a representative contingent of dancers often responded accordingly. He may well have been right about combining
dance music and jazz, for since his first disco/jazz tune appeared on
record in 1975 ("Gwaligo" from *Nucleus*, M-9064), the disco beat has
found its way into the jazz mainstream and still remains a viable

rhythmic influence even today. Rollins's later disco-influenced recordings, "Happy Feel" (*The Way I Feel*, M-9074), "Harlem Boys," and "Disco Monk" (*Don't Ask*, M-9090), are distinct enough to constitute a recognizable tune group.

A much larger category of tune types results from a jazz/rock/funk mix. These usually have simple repetitious, rifflike themes, no bridges or middle sections, and few harmonic progressions. Included among this group are "Lucille" and "Newkleus" (*Nucleus*), "Shout It Out" and "Island Lady" (*The Way I Feel*), "Camel" (*Don't Stop the Carnival*), and many others. The remaining categories are "experiments" of one or two tunes each: "Isn't She Lovely" (*Easy Living*) and "Are You Ready" (*Nucleus*) are rhythm-and-blues tunes—vintage mid-1950s; "Tai-Chi," Rollins's only composition that reflects his long interest in Asian music and culture; and "My Reverie," his only recording from this period based on a classic (Claude Debussy's "Rêverie" for solo piano).

New instrumentation

The personnel of Sonny's groups during the 1970s were as varied as the tunes they performed and recorded. No two successive albums have the same personnel and many differ in instrumentation as well. Some consist of Sonny and rhythm section only (*Sonny Rollins' Next Album*, *Horn Culture*, *The Way I Feel*, *Easy Living*, *Don't Ask*), while others are augmented by horns (*Nucleus* and *Don't Stop the Carnival*). Nearly all have a percussionist who plays primarily conga drums. With the harmonic experiments of the 1960s forgotten, the pianist returns once again as a stable member of Rollins's groups. Keyboard players more than anyone else took advantage of the technicological advances of the late 1960s—the Fender Rhodes electronic piano, synthesizers, and various other electronic keyboards—and as a result became indispensable to the new fusion jazz. Sonny employs several different pianists on his albums of this period and their presence contributes greatly to the overall fusion sound.

Sonny's habit of rotating sidemen contrasts with the other groups of the 1970s, who strived for a more constant personnel and instrumentation in order to achieve some recognizable sound. His preference for experimentation, variety, and change thus led him away from the objectives of most mainstream fusion groups and may help explain his individual approach as a fusion player.

A New Conservatism

Because he appeared to find the independent course that he sought for so long, Rollins's music is more homogeneous during the 1970s than at any other time since his days as a postbop performer. The recordings that follow *Sonny Rollins' Next Album* are similar in content, style, and expression. There are no real musical surprises or radical solutions, only a spirit of mild experimentation tempered by a continuing eclecticism. His improvisations are more sedate now—more references to the themes of tunes and less thematic improvisation.

This new manner of improvising was shaped to some extent by the character of his repertoire. Tunes with fewer harmonic progressions and simpler themes test the creativity of any performer, for the more limited the resources, the more difficult it is to improvise. In the past, Rollins deliberately sought out such tunes ("Wagon Wheels," "I'm an Old Cowhand," "How Are Things in Glocca Morra?" "There's No Business Like Show Business," etc.) for the challenge of making meaningful improvisations from them. Their sparse harmonies allowed him the freedom to create his own, and, on occasion, to venture "outside" the harmonic framework of the tune. In the recordings of the 1970s, however, simple tunes gave rise to a multiplicity of conservative improvisatory styles. In fact, Rollins's recordings of the 1970s are a true compendium of these styles. Some are technically complex and marked by fast-moving, angular, bebop lines. Others are melodically and harmonically static—built on the repetition of a figure, theme, or brief motive. Still others are dominated by nonharmonic squeaks, squeals, and other extramusical sounds; and there are also some instances of inspired melodic playing. But, by far the most striking characteristic of Sonny's improvisations of the 1970s is his tenacious allegiance to the theme. The theme becomes the organizing factor of a large number of his performances as it appears and reappears throughout his improvisations. Some choruses are made up almost entirely of paraphrases of the theme: "First Moves" (*Cutting Edge*), "Island Lady," "Asfrontation Woogie," "Happy Feel," and "Charm Baby" (*The Way I Feel*), "Lucille" (*Nucleus*), "Hear What I'm Saying" (*Easy Living*), and "Harlem Boys" (*Don't Ask*). In others Rollins merely refers to the melody at key points during his improvisations as if to reassure the listener of the identity of the tune.

The technique of repeating the theme differs substantially from his melodic improvisations of the 1950s. Those were true "thematic improvisations"; the theme or portion of it either became the fulcrum for an extended improvisation, or the improvisations made good melodic sense because of a structural similarity with the theme.

Harmony

Rollins's emphasis of the theme in his improvisations was accompanied by a corresponding simplification in the areas of harmony and form. The harmony of jazz had always been the least progressive aspect of the music. With the exception of the modal experiments of the 1960s, jazz harmony had undergone little change since the late 1940s. The chords that served the bebop player did equally well for the improviser of the 1960s, although there were likely to be fewer of them, and the sequence of their progressions was somewhat less predictable. But with the increasing number of jazz originals in the 1970s, and the new virtuosity of the fusion groups, there followed some rapid developments in jazz harmony. Many of the structures from the 1950s and 1960s remained, of course, but to these were added a refined system of chord scales, suspended chords, and an increased use of polytonal harmony. A greater concern for specific bass lines (indicated in jazz "lead sheets" by the placement of bass notes beneath the chords: Bb-/Eb, G-/C, D^9/F# etc.) gave jazz a more linear appearance—a facet of the music that had not been explored since the cool jazz of the 1950s.

Jazz composition, and consequently improvisation, benefited greatly from these improvements to the harmonic system. A body of tunes emerged that were true compositions and not mere formula constructions, as had often been the case in the past. There was less predictability in the harmonic sequences and increased variety on the rhythmic and formal level as well.

Rollins's renewed interest in composing during the 1970s coincides chronologically with this general trend, but with very few exceptions his compositions and improvisations reflect few of the harmonic advances of the other fusion writers. Continuing the trend set by *Sonny Rollins' Next Album*, Rollins's originals divide into modal tunes, tunes constructed on pentatonic scales, blues, and simple functional II—V—I tunes. Most are harmonically static and contain few changes of tonal area.

Tunes constructed from the Dorian mode form the largest identifiable group and include "First Moves" (*The Cutting Edge*), "Sais" (*Horn Culture*), "Gwaligo" (*Nucleus*), "Down the Line," and "Arroz con Pollo" (*Easy Living*). The latter has four measures of Eb Dorian alternating with four measures of Db major plus a bridge. An ostinato bass line is sometimes employed in conjunction with modal harmony to create harmonic tension while reinforcing the tune's structure. "Sais," for example, has a simple two-measure bass ostinato (see example 47) whose steady repetition serves as a great crowd pleaser by building the tension to a high level of excitement.

Example 47. "Sais"

Pentatonic themes and improvisations continue to be a favorite of Rollins's and appear often in combination with modal tunes: "Pictures in the Reflection of a Golden Horn" uses the E-minor pentatonic (E, G, A, B, D), "The Cutting Edge" a pentatonic and A-Mixolydian combination, and "Camel" (*Don't Stop the Carnival*) is constructed on the C-major pentatonic. The Rollins original "Tai-Chi" (*Don't Ask*) contains the most explicit use of the pentatonic scale—its Eastern-sounding melody is constructed exclusively from the notes of the A-major pentatonic (A, B, C#, E, F#—see example 48).

Example 48. "Tai-Chi," 1—4

Pentatonic melodies were even built upon conventional I, VI, IV, V progressions as in "Harlem Boys," which is constructed from the C-minor pentatonic (C, Eb, F, G, Bb—see example 49).

Example 49. "Harlem Boys," 1—3

Rollins continued to record blues tunes during the 1970s, although they are distinguished from earlier performances in this genre by unusual key choices ("Double Feature" [*Love at First Sight*] in A major and "Notes for Eddie" [*Horn Culture*]—a twelve-bar blues in C# minor) or by the lack of a recognizable theme ("Love Man" from *Horn Culture*). In keeping with his conservative stance of the decade, blues resources are kept at a minimum by avoiding substitutions, pedal points, or extended forms and by employing the blues scale as the principal melodic ingredient throughout the improvisations.

Among his compositions, two originals deserve special mention because they digress somewhat from the procedures described above: "Hear What I'm Saying" (*Easy Living*) has an interesting sixteen-measure harmonic pattern and a refreshing change of key before the bass solo. "Don't Ask," one of his best compositions of the decade, contains an interesting harmonic sequence and inspired playing by both himself and guitarist Larry Coryell.

Form

Rollins's indifferent response to the advances of jazz harmony during the 1970s is matched by a use of structurally simple compositions and improvisations. The free jazz of the 1960s severely stymied concern for the form and structure of improvisation; in fact it was the stagnation of the same that had motivated the free jazz experiments in the first place. During the 1970s, pop jazz had an equally negative effect on the goal of musical coherence. As electronic keyboards, gadgets, and extra percussion, coupled with a greater volume level, increased during the 1970s, concern for the melodic and formal integrity of the jazz performance often dwindled. Many jazz performances became heavily amplified "sound experiences" and listeners and musicians alike were enthralled at the vast array of aural possibilities before them. The authentic fusion groups fared better. They went beyond the gadgets and gimmicks to produce, on occasion, a type of highly structured jazz that embodied the time tested musical ingredients of tension and release. Weather Report, Return to Forever, and groups led by Herbie Hancock and others have all contributed structurally imaginative compositions and virtuosic improvisations.

The music of Sonny Rollins, not surprisingly, seems to defy simple classification. The straightforward structure of his compositions and improvisations fits neither in the progressive fusion camp nor in the comfortable world of pop jazz. In fact, attention to musical form seems not to be his concern at all during the 1970s. Beginnings and endings, traditionally the most conspicuous opportunities for some evidence of form or order, are frequently the most unpredictable segments of his performances. Several tunes ("Cosmet," *Nucleus*; "Easy Living," *Easy Living*; "Autumn Nocturne" and "Silver City," *Don't Stop the Carnival*) begin with solo improvisations that appear to be arbitrarily added on, or only remotely connected with, the tune that follows. They are freely improvised, and impressive demonstrations of Rollins's unique ability as a solo performer, but ultimately they merely reaffirm a desire to be sponteneous, and whatever formal sense they embody may be more a result of accident than plan. The introduction to "Swing Low, Sweet Chariot," for example, in which Rollins is joined by Rufus Haley's bagpipes, has more of a formal connection with the tune than most, but only because Haley continues his "droned" interpretation of the tune's theme through the first chorus. (Rollins was trying a lot of things at this time, and the bagpipe introduction was evidently thrown in for effect. Note the audience's enthusiastic approval at the conclusion when the band joins in.)

Rollins is even more unstructured at the endings of tunes. Some end abruptly, as if by chance, on the tonic ("Asfrontation Woogie," "Are You Ready?" "Don't Stop the Carnival," "Everywhere Calypso")—a rare harmonic event in contemporary jazz. Others come to a sudden stop after many repetitions of the theme ("Azalea," "Non-Cents"). For others, the riff-like structure of the theme makes structured endings difficult and they are therefore faded after several repetitions ("Shout It Out," "Pictures in a Reflection of a Golden Horn," "Love Man," "Harlem Boys," "Disco Monk"). Some endings appear totally improvised, with Rollins leading the way and the remainder of the group following. After "Good Morning Heartache" comes to a complete ending, for example, Rollins begins an anticlimactic solo before the trio joins in with a sparse accompaniment. A similar procedure is followed in "To a Wild Rose"—1974 version.

The improvised material in between the beginnings and endings is more structurally predictable when it is based on repetitions of the theme itself (see earlier discussion). But there are also some examples of "outside" playing that seem to hark back to the freer jazz of the 1960s. "Don't Stop the Carnival," "Silver City," and "Autumn Nocturne"—all from *Don't Stop the Carnival*, recorded live in 1978—

contain passages of nonmelodic playing that features extramusical noises and blurred melodic lines unrelated to the harmonic structure of the tunes.

Perhaps because of the increased harmonic and structural resources of the models, or the greater feeling of freedom they allow, in the 1970s Sonny delivers his most structurally cohesive improvisations on other people's compositions. The performances of standards had always been his forte during the years preceding the first retirement, but during the 1960s the excessive freedoms of the avant-garde seemed to diminish his desire to be straightforward. Although he still had not recovered completely in the 1970s, "My One and Only Love" (*Easy Living*) and "To a Wild Rose" (*Cutting Edge*) are refreshing interpretations of these classic ballads, and, in spite of the anticlimactic solo cadenza of the latter, they make more formal sense than the improvisations of his own compositions. Other structurally coherent improvisations can be found in George Duke's "The Way I Feel" and Stanley Clarke's "The Dream That We Fell Out Of," two works that belong more to the mainstream of fusion writing and, perhaps for this reason, offer better opportunities for improvisation.

Critical reaction

Sonny's treatment of form in the 1970s is as casual as his approach to melody or harmony, for all were affected by an overall need for simplicity and directness. The motivation that prompted him to take such an unusual and individual position has perplexed many jazz critics in recent years. As a result, totally favorable reviews of his recordings and live performances have become increasingly rare, and many aspects of his playing have come under attack: the repertoire of tunes, the improvisatory style, and even the quality of his tone.[2] Some critics have also questioned his choice of sidemen, although this has always varied considerably—even during the previous decade.

Apparently unaffected by the criticism, and perhaps even encouraged by the enthusiastic following that he is currently enjoying, Rollins responds philosophically: "I'm still a jazz musician, an improvising jazz musician adding to my storehouse ... and I'm an eclectic player. I like a lot of different styles and would like to bring them all under my umbrella. Perhaps that hasn't happened yet, but that's my aim."

Thus throughout the 1970s, Rollins sought to consolidate his position as a jazz musician through an increasing eclecticism and a continuing search for his niche in the ever-changing environment of contemporary jazz. What had often been a difficult and frustrating struggle for so many years has now stabilized into a steadily productive effort, and one that has not been without its benefits. Today Sonny enjoys an almost unique place among major jazzmen. His reputation as an innovative improviser has given him the freedom to try virtually anything he desires. Few jazz musicians enjoy as enviable a position as he, and even fewer have responded with as individual a solution. Although his "out of step" posture will always subject him to the closest scrutiny of critics and listeners, Rollins's sense of musical integrity remains as firm today as it was thirty years ago, and his spirit of experimentation continues.

10

Summary and Conclusion

For Sonny Rollins, jazz is a continuous pursuit from which one takes periodic breaks and walks away. There is no attainable goal, no end, only a perpetual exercise of discovery and self-renewal. Sonny has no style to sell, no credo to push. His only guide during the past thirty years as an active jazz performer has been his own commitment to experimentation and self-improvement.

Like every other creative jazz musician, Rollins instinctively sought to perfect his skill as an improviser. At times this instinct placed him in the vangauard of developments with unique solutions that were far superior to those of his fellow jazzmen. His success with the technique of thematic improvising culminated a forty-year quest toward that elusive end—one that had been pursued, wittingly or not, by virtually every improvising jazzman since Louis Armstrong. During the late 1950s, when jazz had seemed to reach a static point in its development, he introduced this unique method of improvising based on the theme of the model as well as its harmonic progressions. In doing this, he established melodic unity as the prime structural factor of jazz improvisation. Rollins accomplished this without being bound by the limitations imposed by the tune, and, in addition, was more successful than any other performer in avoiding stereotyped melodic, harmonic, and rhythmic schemes.

His contributions to jazz rhythm, melody, and harmony were modest when compared to his achievements in structuring the continuity of his improvisations, but in each area he improved and refined the system he had inherited from performers before him. His melodies range from complex angular structures to tuneful themes of great lyrical beauty, and his rhythms form a perfect complement to his melodic style. His use of irregular phrasing, frequent rests, and rhythmic patterns that defy accurate transcription into musical notation reveals a truly imaginative rhythmic concept.

Rollins's melodic lines show varying degrees of agreement with the supporting harmonies of the model. While some melodic lines are shaped primarily from chordal tones, others are formed from notes clearly outside the harmonic scheme. Some of these "excursions" are extreme enough to suggest bitonal relationships with the original harmonies of the tune. Rollins was particularly fond of the melodic use of augmented chords and scales, and his employment of diminished scales may be the first consistent use of these structures in the history of jazz improvisation.

In spite of evidence of great formal unity present in his early improvisations, Rollins's structural elements are mosaics of many disparate pieces.[1] Self-deriding quotations of unrelated themes stand side by side with the most inspired and intense motivic and thematic development. Spontaneously conceived lyrical themes, themes related to the model upon which he is improvising, appear and reappear throughout many of his improvisations, structurally binding one segment of an improvisation to another.

Important for the understanding of Rollins's early improvisatory style is the recognition of what he does not play as well as what he does. His skillful paraphrasing of themes and superb sense of timing eliminate much of the redundant element that had characterized the performances of other jazz artists. This is a style of implication rather than direct statement, for Rollins shaped his melodic lines economically, being careful to avoid unnecessary repetition. As a result, a relatively large proportion of his improvisations from this period have an integral "thematic" significance.

During the 1960s and 1970s, Rollins joined movements already in progress, those that were initiated by others, and still managed to make meaningful contributions. Granted, the fruits of those efforts were often controversial, and Rollins received much criticism because of them; but Sonny has never been one to rest on his laurels. The prospect of assuming the position of veteran jazzman by repeating the accomplishments of the 1950s is one he simply could not accept. So, paradoxically, Rollins began abandoning the "thematic" method of improvising soon after returning from a two-year retirement in 1961 without ever fully comprehending the significance of what he had accomplished. Except for a few sporadic efforts in the following years (notably *The Bridge* and to a lesser extent *There Will Never Be Another You*), Rollins's style of the 1960s and 1970s shows an obvious departure from his recordings of the late 1950s. Conspicuously absent in most of the recordings beginning in the early 1960s are the thematic renditions of standards, the type of performance that he had transformed so cleverly into masterpieces of paraphrase and improvisation. In their place Rollins substituted original, but generally simpler, jazz tunes that were less suited to display his ability as a thematic improviser. Not only was the choice of models changed, but, for perhaps the first time in his professional career since he matured as an artist, his playing began to noticeably reflect the influence of other jazz performers. Jazz improvisation in general saw some significant changes during this time, and Rollins's own departure from the traditional mainstream of jazz in the early 1960s coincided with a more general trend in this direction set by others.

Today Rollins continues his search without respect to the traditional boundaries normally observed by most jazzmen. Sonny is freely eclectic now and has been for a number of years; he considers all music, whatever its proximity to jazz, as the raw material for his synthesis, and he actively pursues this synthesis perhaps more thoroughly than any other jazz musician of his generation.

Notes and References

Chapter One

1. The Rollins quotations that appear in this chapter are taken from an interview that took place between the saxophonist and the author on 8 July 1981.

2. Although he occasionally used the nearby Brooklyn Bridge, the Williamsburg was his favorite: "it seemed to have a longer walkway and was more private."

3. Hollie West, "Rollins: Return of a Recluse," *Jazz Forum* 31 (October 1974):23.

4. If the 1955 hospital stay and the trip to India are both included, Rollins's sabbaticals actually total four, not two as usually reported: Lexington sabbatical of 1955; first retirement, 1959—1961; India trip, 1968; and second full sabbatical, 1969—1971.

Chapter Two

1. Frank Tirro, "Constructive Elements in Jazz Improvisation," *Journal of the American Musicological Society* (Summer 1974):285.

2. Ronald Byrnside, "The Performer as Creator: Jazz Improvisation," in *Contemporary Music and Music Cultures*, ed. Byrnside, Charles Hamm, and Bruno Nettl (Englewood Cliffs, N.J., 1975), p. 224.

3. Willi Apel, "Improvisation," in *Harvard Dictionary of Music*, 2d Ed. (Cambridge, Mass., 1969), p. 404.

4. Tirro, "Constructive Elements," p. 287.

5. See Tirro's persuasive argument concerning this claim; ibid., p. 297 ff.

6. See Avril Dankworth, *Jazz: An Introduction to Its Musical Basis* (London, 1968), pp. 16—17, and Gunther Schuller, "Sonny Rollins and Thematic Improvising," in *Jazz Panorama*, ed. Martin Williams (New York, 1964), pp. 239—40.

7. This differs from earlier jazz, where the endings are often abruptly truncated or did not return to a complete statement the original theme. See "Wrappin It Up" (Fletcher Henderson); "Grandpa's Spells" (Jelly Roll Morton); "Body and Soul" and "The Man I Love" (Coleman Hawkins), and others in *The Smithsonian Collection of Classic Jazz*, selected and annotated by Martin Williams (Washington, D.C.: The Smithsonian Institution, 1973).

8. For an account of this rather complex procedure, see Frank Tirro, "The Silent Theme Tradition in Jazz," *Musical Quarterly* 53 (July 1967):313—34.

9. Gillespie and Parker's "Anthropology" originated in this manner. See Leonard Feather, *Inside Jazz* (New York, 1977), p. 59.

10. For an illuminating account of how jazz communicates to its audience, see Alan P. Merriam, "The Jazz Community," *Social Forces* 38 (1960):211—22.

11. Schuller, "Sonny Rollins and Thematic Improvising," p. 252.

Chapter Three

1. One of the more difficult concepts to define in discussions concerning jazz, "swing," for our purposes, refers to a forward-moving rhythmic sensation whereby a certain momentum is collectively achieved by the ensemble. The feeling of swing contributes to the ease and spontaneity of the jazz performance.

2. See Gunther Schuller, *Early Jazz: Its Roots and Musical Development* (New York, 1968), p. 180.

3. A "changing note" is the tone that moves or literally "changes" in a progression of two chords having the majority of their notes in common. Bb, for example, is the changing note in a progression of C major to C dominant seventh. The practice of emphasizing the flat seventh of a dominant-seventh chord is possibly a carryover from Armstrong's function as second cornet with King Oliver. In classic New Orleans Dixieland, a secondary melodic instrument (usually the trombone) would sound the flat seventh when a chord changed from a simple triad to the dominant seventh in the fourth measure of the blues.

4. An interesting juxtaposition of older and newer styles occurs in the 1960 recording *Night Hawk* (Prestige 7671), which features, along with Hawkins, the younger saxophonist Eddie "Lockjaw" Davis. In his phrasing, repertoire of sounds, and use of syncopated rhythmic accents, the latter player reveals the extent to which jazz had progressed since the 1930s. Hawkins, by contrast, is clearly of a different generation, clinging to the older, more regularly accented downbeat style. See especially "There Is No Greater Love," and "Pedalin'."

5. Quoted from Jon Newsom, "Jazz: Aspects of Melodic Improvisation," in *Music in the Modern Age*, The Praeger History of Western Music, F. W. Sternfeld, general ed. (New York, 1973), p. 403.

6. The failure to resolve the dissonance conventionally may be the basis of complaints by some that they hear wrong notes in bebop. See Feather, *Inside Jazz*, pp. 69—70.

7. Owens divides the motives into chromatic and chordal categories, and further classifies them according to the harmonic framework in which they are used, the pitch (chord member or scale degree) which they encircle, and their frequency of occurrence. See Thomas Owens, "Charlie Parker: Techniques of Improvisation" (Ph.D. Diss., University of California, Los Angeles, 1974), vol. 1. Chapter 3, and vol. 2, pp. 1—10.

8. Quoted from Nat Hentoff, "An Afternoon with Miles Davis," in *Jazz Panorama*, p. 167.

Chapter Four

1. Gordon Kopulos, "Needed Now: Sonny Rollins," *Downbeat*, 24 June 1971, p. 13.

2. When citing examples in the recordings of Rollins, the Roman numeral identifies Rollins's improvised chorus and the arabic numeral(s) refers to measure numbers. The designation "St. Thomas," I, 1—8, for example, refers to measures 1 through 8 of Rollins's first improvised chorus of that tune. All tenor saxophone transcriptions are transposed up one octave.

Chapter Five

1. The symbols used to represent the various chord types are similar to those used in Jamey Aebersold, *A New Approach to Jazz Improvisation* (New Albany, Ind., 1974), 3:1. They represent a consensus of the most common symbols used in jazz harmony and may be interpreted as follows:

CΔ	— a major scale/chord, emphasizing the major seventh and major ninth.
C-, C-7	— minor triad or minor-seventh chord (minor triad with a minor seventh).
C-7(b5), C07	— diminished triad with a minor-seventh or half-diminished-seventh chord.
C^7	— dominant-seventh chord.
C^7(sus^4)	— dominant-seventh chord with a suspended fourth.
C^7(b5, +5)	— dominant-seventh chord with altered fifths.
C^7(b9, +9)	— dominant-seventh chord with altered ninths. (also applied to altered elevenths and thirteenths).
C^0	— diminished triad
C^{07}	— diminished-seventh chord
C+, C+^{7}	— augmented triad, dominant-seventh chord with raised fifth.

Other symbols used:

( )	— indicates "ghosting" of note, i.e., note gets less emphasis.
(~~~~)	— denotes a passage that, for reasons of intonation or dominant background accompaniment, cannot be notated exactly.
- - - - - -	— indicates a passage where the soloist "lags behind" the rhythm section's beat.
/ or \	— Slurs of indeterminate pitch from one note to another.
x	— Note of indefinite pitch.

2. In jazz harmony, an extended chord is one containing a ninth, eleventh, or thirteenth or any of their chromatically altered members (augmented or flatted ninths, the augmented eleventh or the flatted thirteenth). The extensions beyond the ninth and their chromatic alterations were most often applied to the dominant-seventh-type chords.

3. Byrnside, "The Performer as Creator: Jazz Improvisation," p. 236.

4. See Schuller, *Early Jazz*, p. 83.

5. For a more detailed analysis of "Blue Seven," see Schuller, "Sonny Rollins and Thematic Improvising," pp. 241—50.

6. Additional examples of diminished scales can be found in the recordings "Blue Seven" (the first three measures of the theme are based on a half-step/whole-step diminished scale on Bb); Rollins also builds much of the eighth and ninth choruses on these structures.

Chapter Six

1. See Owens, "Charle Parker: Techniques of Improvisation," 2:1—10.

2. Schuller, "Sonny Rollins and Thematic Improvising," p. 247.

Chapter Seven

1. See Frank Kofsky, *Black Nationalism and the Revolution in Music* (New York, 1970), pp. 125—44.

Chapter Eight

1. J. R. Taylor, on the jacket notes for *Green Dolphin Street* (a reissue of *On Impulse* [Impulse A-91]), for example, makes too strong a case for this album belonging to Rollins's "post—avant-garde" period; Rollins was still performing in the free jazz vein when this recording was made.

Chapter Nine

1. See transcription by Charley Gerard, *Sonny Rollins* (New York, 1980), pp. 35—37.

2. Some of the recent reviews that have not been entirely favorable include John Litweiler, review of *Nucleus* (recording, Milestone M-9064), in *Downbeat*, 8 April 1976, p. 20; Charles Suber, "The First Chorus," *Downbeat*, 7 April 1977, p. 6; and Bill Kirchner, "Caught in the Act," a review of a live performance in Silver Spring, Maryland, *Downbeat*, 2 June 1977, p. 37.

Chapter Ten

1. So varied and even incongruous are Rollins's basic improvisatory materials that his success in combining them to form coherent musical statements seems all the more remarkable. In this light, Gushee refers to him as "a Romantic who has a sense of the 'glory of the imperfect.'" See Larry Gushee, "Sonny Rollins," in *Jazz Panorama*, p. 254.

Selected Bibliography

1. Books

Aebersold, Jamey. *A New Approach to Jazz Improvisation*. New Albany, Ind.: Jamey Aebersold, 1979. Vol. 1, 39 pp., vol 8, 32 pp. This is an excellent "play-along" series of twenty-six volumes, complete with records and instruction booklets. Volume 1 introduces the melodic, harmonic, and rhythmic materials of improvisation; volume 8 contains the "lead sheets" for eight Rollins originals.

Baker, David. *The Jazz Style of Sonny Rollins*. Lebanon, Ind.: Studio 224, 1980, 108 pp. Nine of Rollins's performances are transcribed and analyzed on "analysis sheets." The analyses are vague and inconclusive, but the discography and bibliography contain useful information.

Berendt, Joachim-Ernst. *The Jazz Book*. New York: Lawrence Hill, 1975, 459 pp. This is an historical survey of jazz from the beginnings to the 1970s. The orientation is toward early jazz—only pp. 382—93 are devoted to postbop developments.

Brown, Ray, and Brown, Steve. *An Introduction to Jazz Improvisation*. New York: Piedmont Music Co., 1975. 48 pp. This one-volume "play-along" record and booklet contains accurate basic theory information and eleven exercises on which to practice. Explanations are minimal; the emphasis is on performing with the recordings.

Budds, Michael J. *Jazz in the Sixties*. Iowa City: Union of Iowa Press, 1978. 124 pp. The author has compiled an excellent analytical study of the 1960s: how jazz developed to this point and its future directions. An extensive bibliography and discography are included.

Coker, Jerry C. *Improvising Jazz*. Englewood Cliffs, N.J.: Prentice-Hall, 1964. 115 pp. Formerly the author's master's thesis, this is a pioneering study on the materials of improvisation. Particularly useful are the chapters on the diminished scale, chord superimposition, functional harmony, and the tables of common chord progressions. Because of the early publication date, discussions are limited to standard tunes and blues.

Cole, Bill. *Miles Davis: A Musical Biography*. New York: William Morrow and Co., 1974. 256 pp. This study provides detailed information on the career of Davis, one of the most influential and yet mysterious figures of modern jazz, but contains obvious errors in the transcriptions (pitch and bar-line placement). Both the bibliography and discography appear to be complete.

Dankworth, Avril. *Jazz, An Introduction to Its Musical Basis*. London: Oxford University Press, 1968. 89 pp. For a brief introduction, this book is accurate and straightforward. The limitations of length do not allow the author much depth in the discussions. Appendixes of standard tunes and discography are included.

Davis, Nathan. *Writings in Jazz.* 2d ed. Dubuque, Iowa: Gorsuch, Scarisbrick, 1978. 172 pp. This is not a collection of writings on jazz, as the title implies, but a survey of jazz styles with the emphasis on the contributions of black musicians. An informative chapter on the avant-garde (pp. 125—34) is included.

Feather, Leonard. *Inside Jazz.* New York: Da Capo Press, 1977, 103 pp. This reprint of *Inside Bebop* (New York: J. J. Robbins, 1949) is an excellent study of the beginnings of modern jazz. Section 2 ("How," pp. 49—72) is particularly valuable as an introduction to the musical workings of bebop. A new introduction by the author is included.

Gerard, Charley. *Sonny Rollins.* New York: Consolidated Music Publishing, 1980. 72 pp. Eight of Rollins's recorded solos, most from the 1970s, are transcribed and analyzed. A section called "Analysis of Rollins's Style" (pp. 40—71) tabulates the harmonic, melodic, and formal structure of Rollins's music, but draws no conclusions about his contribution as an improviser.

Gitler, Ira. *Jazz Masters of the Forties.* New York: Macmillan and Co., 1966. 290 pp. This study has nine chapters devoted to the innovators of the 1940s including Charlie Parker, Dizzy Gillespie, Bud Powell, J. J. Johnson, Kenny Clarke, and others. A discography is provided at the end of each chapter.

Goldberg, Joe. *Jazz Masters of the Fifties.* New York: Macmillan and Co., 1965, 246 pp. This has the same format as the publication above and contains a chapter on Rollins. A discography of each musician discussed is provided.

Gridley, Mark. *Jazz Styles.* Englewood Cliffs, N.J.: Prentice-Hall, 1978. 409 pp. This jazz-appreciation text is weighted toward the modern period. Included are chapters on Ornette Coleman, Charles Mingus, John Coltrane, and Miles Davis. A glossary of terms and an annotated discography are also provided.

Harrison, Max. *Charlie Parker.* New York: Barnes and Co., 1961. 84 pp. Parker's career is traced in this brief account that includes information on his Kansas City background, his early years as a sideman, and his achievements as a mature jazz artist. There are no analyses or musical examples; pages 75 through 84 are devoted to discography.

Hentoff, Nat, and McCarthy, Albert J., ed. *Jazz: New Perspectives on the History of Jazz.* New York: Grove Press, 1961. 387 pp. Twelve scholars write on various aspects of jazz. Martin Williams contributes "Bebop and After"; Max Harrison, "Charlie Parker"; and Franklin S. Driggs, "Kansas City and the Southwest."

Hodeir, André. *Jazz: Its Evolution and Its Essence.* Translated by David Noakes. New York: Grove Press, 1956. 295 pp. This early analytical study contains three chapters on the modern period: chapter 7, "Charlie Parker and the Bebop Movement," pp. 99—115; Chapter 8, "Miles Davis and the Cool Tendency," pp. 116—38; and Chapter 9, "Melody in Jazz," pp. 139—57.

James, Michael. *Miles Davis.* New York: A. S. Barnes and Co. Inc., 1961. 90 pp. Davis's career is traced in this brief biographical account. Pages 81 through 90 contain a discography of early Davis recordings from 1945— 1959.

Jones, Leroi. *Black Music.* New York: William Morrow and Co., 1968. 221 pp. This is a collection of essays, reviews, interviews, liner notes, musical analyses, and personal impressions on black jazz musicians, written between 1959—1967. The seventh essay is a review of Rollins's *Our Man in Jazz* (RCA LPM-2612) written in 1964.

————. *Blues People: Negro Music in White America.* New York: William Morrow and Co., 1963. 244 pp. Jones discusses jazz and the blues in the context of American social history: the development of black music and values that affected white America. Chapter 12, "The Modern Scene," describes the impact of bebop and modern jazz on American society.

Kofsky, Frank. *Black Nationalism and the Revolution in Music.* New York: Pathfinder Press, 1970. 280 pp. The author presents an historical account of the avant-garde revolution of the 1960s. Considerable emphasis is given to the role of John Coltrane, his followers, and sidemen, with chapters on Coltrane, Elvin Jones, McCoy Tyner, and Albert Ayler.

Mehegan, John. *Jazz Improvisation.* 4 vols. New York: Watson-Guptill, 1965. This is a comprehensive analytical study of jazz improvisation in four volumes: 1. Tonal and Rhythmic Principles; 2. Jazz Rhythm and the Improvised Line; 3. Swing and Early Progressive Piano Styles; and 4. Contemporary Piano Styles. Included are the harmonic progressions to many standard tunes, and transcriptions of jazz solos by Coleman Hawkins, Bix Beiderbecke, Charlie Parker, Art Tatum, and many others.

Moon, Pete, comp., and Witherden, Barry, ed. *A Bibliography of Jazz Discographies Published Since 1960.* London: British Institute of Jazz Studies Project, ca. 1969. 32 pp. This is an extensive listing of discographies of prominent jazz artists. Many appear in jazz periodicals.

Ostransky, Leroy. *The Anatomy of Jazz.* Seattle: University of Washington Press, 1960. 362 pp. The author introduces jazz as "serious" music and surveys each period. Chapters are devoted to the understanding of jazz (musical elements, etc.) and the various styles through bebop.

Reisner, Robert. *Bird: The Legend of Charlie Parker.* New York: Citadel Press, 1962. 256 pp. Reisner pieces together a portrait of Parker and his effect on a whole generation of musicians through reminiscences collected from eighty-one interviews. Among those providing accounts are Max Roach, Charles Mingus, Jay McShann, Mrs. Addie Parker (his mother), Miles Davis, and Dizzy Gillespie.

Russell, Ross. *Jazz Styles in Kansas City and the Southwest.* Berkeley: University of California Press, 1971. 292 pp. This is the first full-length historical study of Kansas City as an important center for jazz after New Orleans and Chicago. There are entire chapters on Charlie Parker, Lester Young, Count Basie, and Bennie Moten, but no musical examples.

Sargeant, Winthrop. *Jazz: Hot and Hybrid.* New York: E. P. Dutton and Co., 1946. 287 pp. The author presents an excellent analytical introduction to the basic elements of early jazz: its rhythm, melody, and harmony.

Schuller, Gunther. *Early Jazz: Its Roots and Musical Development.* New York: Oxford University Press, 1968. 401 pp. This is the first systematic, comprehensive history that deals with the specifics of the music. The first of a two-volume set, only jazz through the mid-1930s is covered. There are chapters on the origins of jazz, Louis Armstrong, Jelly Roll Morton, and Duke Ellington and a selected discography (pp. 385—389).

Stearns, Marshall W. *The Story of Jazz.* New York: Oxford University Press, 1970. 272 pp. The author presents a scholarly and well-documented, comprehensive history. The 1958 edition contains a syllabus of lectures on the history of jazz.

Tirro, Frank. *Jazz: A History.* New York: W. W. Norton, 1977. 457 pp. This is a comprehensive survey of jazz, the first to go through the modern period, that focuses on the music itself. There are many musical examples, transcriptions of famous solos, and a selected discography of 100 albums illustrating the history of jazz.

Williams, Martin, ed. *The Art of Jazz.* New York: Oxford University Press, 1959. 248 pp. Williams assembles a collection of essays, some of which are on the modern period: "Bebop" (Ross Russell, pp. 187—214) and "The Funky Hard Bop Regression" (Martin Williams, pp. 233—38).

————. *Jazz Panorama.* New York: Collier Books, 1964. 318 pp. This valuable anthology represents a selection of articles, interviews, and reviews from the *Jazz Review.* Included are Nat Hentoff, "An Afternoon With Miles Davis," pp. 161—68; Dick Katz, "Miles Davis," pp. 169—79; Ross Russell, "Charlie Parker and Dizzy Gillespie," pp. 180—86; Gunther Schuller, "Sonny Rollins and Thematic Improvising," pp. 139—252; and Larry Gushee, "Sonny Rollins," pp. 253—57.

Wilson, John S. *Jazz: The Transition Years, 1940—1960.* New York: Appleton-Century-Crofts, 1966. 185 pp. The author gives an historical account of the development of modern jazz and its acceptance as world music. Pertinent chapters include "Jazz Around the World" and "Jazz and the Mass Audience."

2. Parts of Books

Byrnside, Ronald. "The Performer as Creator: Jazz Improvisation." In: Charles Hamm, Bruno Nettl, and Ronald Byrnside. *Contemporary Music and Music Cultures,* pp. 223—51. Englewood Cliffs, N.J.: Prentice-Hall, 1975. 270 pp. This article makes some perceptive distinctions between jazz and "fixed" music and contains a well-presented explanation of jazz improvisation.

Hentoff, Nat. "An Afternoon with Miles Davis." In: *Jazz Panorama.* Edited by Martin Williams, pp. 161—68. New York: Collier Books, 1964. 318 pp. Miles Davis reacts to other jazz musicians' recordings. Of particular interest is his preference for sparse harmonic accompaniments and backgrounds—ideas that permeate his music of the 1960s.

Newsom, Jon. "Jazz: Aspects of Melodic Improvisation." In: *Music in the Modern Age.* F. W. Sternfeld, general editor, pp. 395—406. New York: Praeger and Co., 1973. 515 pp. This general introduction to melodic improvisation is based on the recordings of Louis Armstrong, Lester Young, and Lennie Tristano. A chart outlining the history of jazz from 1900 to 1971 appears on pp. 400—401.

Schuller, Gunther. "Sonny Rollins and Thematic Improvising." In: *Jazz Panorama*. Edited by Martin Williams, pp. 239—52. New York: Collier Books, 1964. 318 pp. This article contains Schuller's much-discussed analysis of Rollins's "Blue Seven." The author concludes that Rollins is fundamentally different from other jazz improvisers because of his melodic approach.

————. "Thelonious Monk." In: *Jazz Panorama*, pp. 216—38. Monk's early recordings are surveyed and selections from thirteen LPs are discussed in terms of his singular approach to improvising.

Work, John Wesley. "Jazz." In: *Harvard Dictionary of Music*. 2d ed. Edited by Willi Apel, pp. 440—44. Cambridge: The Belknap Press, 1969. 935 pp. The author gives the traditional academic view of jazz, described in terms of European art music. Many errors are made in explaining the musical workings of jazz.

3. Articles

Avakian, George. "Sonny Meets Hawk and How It Happened." *Jazz* 2 (October 1963):17. The author tells of the joint performance of Rollins and Coleman Hawkins at the 1963 Newport Jazz Festival and how it led to the RCA recording *Sonny Meets Hawk* (RCA 741074/075).

Berg, Chuck. "Sonny Rollins: The Way Newk Feels." *Downbeat*, 7 April 1977, pp. 13—14, 38—41. In this article based on an interview, Rollins discusses his musical philosophy and compositional techniques.

Carno, Zita. "The Style of John Coltrane." Part 1, *Jazz Review* 2 (October 1959):17—21; Part 2 (November 1959):pp. 13—17. This superficial analysis of Coltrane's pre-avant-garde style contains some transcriptions of his music, including a complete transcription of "Blue Train."

Feather, Leonard. "Rollins in 3/4 Time." *Downbeat*, 12 December 1957, p. 39. Rollins reacts to ten jazz-waltz recordings in a "Blindfold Test" and gives a good glimpse of his musical personality.

Fiofori, Tam. "Re-entry: The New Orbit of Sonny." *Downbeat*, 14 October 1971, pp. 14—15, 39. The author quizzes Rollins on his activities of the past few years, his involvement with free jazz, the "bridge" sabbatical, and his interest in Eastern religion and philosophy.

Gitler, Ira. "Bird and the Forties." *Downbeat*, 2 July 1964, pp. 32—36, 97—98. Gitler discusses Parker's role in the bop revolution of the 1940s, and his influence on the musicians who came after him.

Goldberg, Joe. "The Further Adventures of Sonny Rollins." *Downbeat*, 26 August 1965, pp. 19—21. This is an account of Rollins's appearance at the Village Vanguard. The author provides insight concerning Rollins's musical philosophy and the events surrounding the concert, but makes no criticisms of his performance.

Haddock, Dick. "Freedom Suite." *Jazz Review* 2 (May 1959):10—11. The author examines Rollins's only effort at an extended composition and declares it a success because "it requires and generates spontaneous collective and individual improvisation."

Hentoff, Nat. "Sonny Rollins." *Downbeat*, 28 November 1956, pp. 15—16. Hentoff gives a good summary of Rollins's career to date: how he began, his early interest in music, and his beginnings with Miles Davis, Clifford Brown, and Max Roach.

Hoefer, George. "Coleman Hawkins' Pioneer Days." *Downbeat*, 5 October 1967, pp. 20—22. This is a short but detailed account of Hawkins's early career and how he transformed the saxophone into a "serious jazz instrument."

James, Michael. "Sonny Rollins on Record, 1949—54." *Jazz Monthly* 5 (October 1959):7—11. James's evaluation of Rollins's progress toward maturity in his early recordings provides some valuable information on recording dates and personnel.

Jeske, Lee. "Sonny Rollins: The Greatest Jazz Soloist Alive Today." *Jazz Journal International* 32 (January 1979):56. The author discusses the incompatibility of Rollins and McCoy Tyner in their recent "White House All-Star" collaboration and declares Rollins still the master of the unaccompanied solo.

Jones, Max. "A Personal Portrait of Sonny Rollins." *Melody Maker*, 16 November 1968, p. 12. Jones describes a recent documentary on Rollins aired on BBC 2 entitled "Sonny Rollins, Musician."

Kofsky, Frank. "The Jazz Scene." *Jazz* 6 (February 1967):22—23. The author questions the suitability of jazz night clubs as an appropriate setting for artistic creation.

———. "John Coltrane and the Jazz Revolution: The Case of Albert Ayler." *Jazz* 9 (September 1966):24—25; 10 (October 1966):20—22. This is an account of John Coltrane's influence on the younger revolutionary Albert Ayler.

———. "Return of Sonny." *Jazz Journal* 15 (May 1962):12—14. Rollins's appearance at the Renaissance in Los Angeles provides an opportunity for this interview. The author probes Rollins's reactions to other musicians, especially John Coltrane and Ornette Coleman, and his ideas concerning thematic improvisation.

Kopulos, Gordon. "Needed Now: Sonny Rollins." *Downbeat*, 24 June 1971. pp. 12—13, 30. This flattering article praises Rollins's accomplishments of the 1950s and 1960s and looks forward to his return from retirement.

Korall, Burt. "My Exile Has Paid Off." *Melody Maker*, 23 December 1961, p. 7. Rollins discusses the reasons for his first sabbatical and the musical benefits derived from it.

Merriam, Alan P., and Mack, Raymond W. "The Jazz Community." *Social Forces* 38 (1960):211—22. The jazz musician, his listeners, and followers are examined as isolated members of American society.

Morgenstern, Dan. "Coleman Hawkins, 1904—1969," *Downbeat*, 26 June 1969, pp. 13—14. This brief sketch of Hawkins's career list most of his important recordings including *Sonny Meets Hawk* (RCA LPM 2712).

Porter, Bob. "This Man Called Sonny Rollins." *Downbeat*, 14 February 1974, pp. 14—15. The author gives a very broad appraisal of Rollins's career during the 1970s and includes a discography.

Priestly, Brian. "Max Roach and Sonny at Reading." *Jazz Monthly* 12 (January 1967):11—12. Priestly describes a performance of Rollins at the University of Reading on 6 November 1966. The author gives a minute-by-minute account of a typical Rollins set as he heard it.

Primack, Bret. "Sonny Rollins: The Way He Feels." *Downbeat*, 25 January 1979, pp. 12—13. In this interview, Rollins comments on his new eclecticism and independence from mainstream jazz.

Schuller, Gunther. "Future of Form in Jazz." *Saturday Review* 40 (12 January 1957):62—63, 67—68. Schuller speculates on the possibilities offered by extended form and the advances made by Jimmy Guiffre, George Russell, Ellington, and Parker.

Scott, Ronnie. "The Verdict on Sonny Rollins." *Melody Maker*, 13 February 1965, p. 10. This article records the British reaction to the "new" Sonny Rollins of the avant-garde period.

Stewart, Zan. "Sonny Rollins: A Restless Searcher." *International Musician and Recording World* 4 (May 1980):36—39, 41. Information on some of Rollins's more recent activities is contained in this brief biographical sketch.

Suber, Charles. "The First Chorus." *Downbeat*, 7 April 1977, p. 6. The author speculates on Rollins's motives for his apparent move toward pop/jazz.

Tirro, Frank. "Constructive Elements in Jazz Improvisation." *Journal of the American Musicological Society* 27 (Summer 1974):285—306. This penetrating analytical study describes in detail the process of jazz improvisation and contains transcriptions of recorded solos by Clifford Brown, Charlie Parker, and Ornette Coleman.

———. "The Silent Theme Tradition in Jazz." *Music Quarterly* 53 (July 1967):313—34. This informative discussion describes the process whereby standard tunes are transformed into vehicles for bebop improvisation. The musical examples are well chosen and the commentary is excellent.

Wang, Richard. "Jazz circa 1945: A Confluence of Styles." *Musical Quarterly* 59 (October 1973):531—46. The author analyzes the differences between swing and bebop and describes the process of jazz improvisation in terms of its internal logic and cohesiveness.

Weiss, David. "The Self-Renewing Sonny Rollins." *Jazz Magazine* 4 (Spring 1980): 66—73. The information in this article is based on an interview in which Rollins discusses his changes in style and his recent inactivity.

West, Hollie. "Rollins: Return of a Recluse." *Jazz Forum* 31 (October 1974):21—24. This biographical sketch provides some new information on Rollins's activities during his sabbaticals.

Wild, David. "Woodshed: Sonny Rollins's Solo on 'Pent-Up House.'" *Jazz Magazine* 4 (Spring 1980):74—76. The author analyzes his own transcription of "Pent-Up House" but with some melodic and rhythmic errors and a misunderstanding of the 32-bar form.

Williams, Martin. "Coleman Hawkins, Some Notes on a Phoenix." *Jazz Journal* 21 (January 1968):6—7. Williams reflects on the career and contribution of Hawkins and briefly describes the significance of his more important recordings.

———. "Extended Improvisation and Form: Some Solutions." *Jazz Review* 1 (December 1958):13—15, 49. The author discusses the treatment of form by various jazz artists including Sonny Rollins, and concludes that Rollins has laid the foundation for the extended solo in the modern idiom.

———. "Ornette Coleman: Ten Years After." *Downbeat*, Part 1, 25 December 1969, pp. 24—25; Part 2, 8 January 1970, pp. 9, 33—34. This is a good analytical study of Ornette Coleman with examples drawn primarily from his early recordings. A discography of early recordings is provided.

———. "Rollins and Davis Reviewed." *Saturday Review* 48 (30 October 1965):91. Williams laments Rollins's involvement with "the new thing" (free jazz), but views *On Impulse* (A-91) as a return to his former melodic style.

Zabor, Rafi. "Let Us Now Praise Sonny Rollins." *Musician, Player and Listener* 23 (March 1980):38—43. The author explores the Rollins charisma and comments favorably on his recordings of the 1960s and 1970s.

4. Encyclopedias

Feather, Leonard. "The Anatomy of Jazz." In: *The New Edition of The Encyclopedia of Jazz*. New York: Horizon Press, 1960, pp. 60—78. The melody, harmony, and rhythm of bebop are discussed in terms of their departure from earlier jazz styles. Many good musical examples and illustrations are included.

———. "Jazz in American Society." In: *The New Edition of The Enclopedia of Jazz*. New York: Horizon Press, 1960, pp. 79—88. Feather presents an illuminating discussion of jazz musicians as forming a subculture in the United States.

———. *The Encyclopedia of Jazz in the Sixties*. New York: Horizon Press, 1966. 312 pp. This volume updates the earlier *The New Edition of The Encyclopedia of Jazz* with current entries and a new introduction. "The Practitioner as Preacher: The Best of the Blindfold Test" (pp. 22—31) records musicians' reactions to recordings of their peers from this period.

———, and Gitler, Ira. *The Encyclopedia of Jazz in the 1970s*. New York: Horizon Press, 1976. 393 pp. Additions to the earlier editions are included, along with an "Introduction" by Quincy Jones (pp. 12—14) and a new "Blindfold Test" (pp. 15—35).

5. Reviews

Bouchard, Fred. "Sonny's Back to Stay." *Melody Maker,* 1 December 1973, p. 24. Rollins's appearance at Boston's Jazz Workshop is reviewed favorably, but not analytically.

Gushee, Larry. "Sonny Rollins." In *Jazz Panorama*. Edited by Martin Williams. New York: Collier Books, 1964, pp. 253—57. The recording

Sonny Rollins and the Big Brass is reviewed by Gushee, who follows the lead of Gunther Schuller in analyzing the formal attributes of Rollins's playing.

Katz, Dick. "Miles Davis." In: *Jazz Panorama*. Edited by Martin Williams. New York: Collier Books, 1964, pp. 169—79. This review is one of the few developed pieces of criticism on the early recordings of Miles Davis. The recordings reviewed are *Bag's Groove* (Prestige 7109), *Walkin'* (Prestige 7076), and *Bemsha Swing* (Prestige 10" 196).

Kirchner, Bill. "Caught in the Act." *Downbeat*, 2 June 1977, p. 37. This is an unfavorable review of Rollins's appearance at the Showboat Lounge in Silver Spring, Maryland. The exact date of the performance is not given.

Litweiler, John. "Nucleus." *Downbeat*, 8 April 1976, p. 20. The reviewer questions Rollins's motivation in his recent recordings.

McDonough, John. "Saxophone Collossus and More" and "The Bridge." *Downbeat*, 11 September 1975, p. 24. In reviewing these two albums, the author compares the Rollins of the 1950s with his new, changed position of the 1960s, but fails adequately to describe the change.

Palmer, Richard. "Next Album," "Horn Culture," and "The Cutting Edge." *Jazz Journal* 29 (May 1976):38. This flattering and uncritical review reveals that Rollins has a following among critics in spite of his fluctuating musical philosophy.

Russell, Ross. "Charlie Parker and Dizzy Gillespie." In: *Jazz Panorama*. Edited by Martin Williams. New York: Collier Books, 1964, pp. 180—86. The author, a former proprietor of Dial Records who recorded Parker in the 1940s, reviews three vintage recordings and offers insights on the relationship between Parker and Gillespie.

Stern, Chip. "Don't Stop the Carnival." *Jazz Magazine* 1 (Fall 1978):62. Stern likes everything about this album and claims that reports of Rollins's demise are exaggerated.

6. Record Jacket Notes

Avakian, George. *The Bridge*. RCA APL1-0859. The author explains the significance of the title of this album and gives a brief description of each selection on the recording.

———. *Sonny Meets Hawk*. RCA LPM 2712. Remarks are made about Rollins's growing tendency toward free jazz. Brief descriptions of each selection are included.

———. *What's New?* RCA LPM 2572 This is a very flattering but shallow explanation of the album's contents. The author incorrectly uses the term "bossa nova" to describe some of the selections.

Blumenthal, Bob. *Sonny Rollins: More From the Vanguard*. The Blue Note Reissue Series. BN LA 475 H2. The author gives biographical backgrounds on each of the sidemen and discusses Rollins's sense of humor in his playing.

Davis, Brian. Sonny Rollins: *Tenor Titan*. Verve 2683 054. The individual selections, assembled from several different recording sessions, are briefly described.

Fox, Charles. *The Freedom Suite Plus*. Milestone 47007. The author places Rollins's contributions in historical perspective and provides a brief formal analysis of "The Freedom Suite."

Hentoff, Nat. *Thelonious Monk: Brilliance*. Milestone M-47023. Hentoff provides many details on the erratic career of Monk and comments on the unorthodoxy of his style.

Keepnews, Orrin. *Don't Stop the Carnival*. Milestone M 55005. This is a very brief account of the circumstances that led to the making of the recording and reveals Rollins's casual manner in planning his music.

Palmer, Robert. *Saxophone Colossus and More*. Prestige P-24050. Rollins's reaction to Schuller's analysis of "Blue Seven" is included in this brief biographical sketch.

———. *Sonny Rollins*. Blue Note BN LA 401-H2. Palmer recounts the usual events in Rollins's career and provides descriptions, more detailed than usual, of the individual tunes.

Taylor, J. R. *Sonny Rollins: Green Dolphin Street*. Quintessence QJ-25181. The author gives a brief summary of Rollins's styles up to the mid-1970s, but mistakenly labels this recording (a reprint of Impulse A-91) as "post-avant-garde" when, in fact, it is a continuation of Rollins's free style.

Williams, Martin. *The Smithsonian Collection of Classic Jazz*. Washington, D.C.: The Smithsonian Associates and W. W. Norton, 1973. 46 pp. The accompanying booklet for this outstanding anthology of recordings defines jazz, outlines the principal style periods, and provides valuable discographical and critical information on the selections. The emphasis is on jazz before 1960.

7. Dissertations

Baskerville, Davis. "The Influence of Jazz on Art Music to Mid-Century." University of California, Los Angeles, 1965. 535 pp. (Microfilm. Ann Arbor: University Microfilms.) This study seeks to determine the influence of jazz on European and American art music from 1900 to 1950. Jazz rhythm, melody, harmony, timbre, and texture are defined and distinctions are made among jazz, popular, commercial, and art music.

Hansen, Chadwicke Clarke. "The Ages of Jazz: A Study of Jazz in Its Cultural Context." University of Minnesota, 1956. 213 pp. (Microfilm. Ann Arbor: University Microfilms.) This is a study of the cultural environment in which jazz grew with emphasis on the early years. The author concludes that jazz moved from the status of a folk art to a "high art" with a body of formal criticism and consciousness of its own past.

Owens, Thomas. "Charlie Parker: Techniques of Improvisation." University of California, Los Angeles, 1974. Volume 1, 385 pp., Volume 2, 478 pp. (Xerox copy. Ann Arbor: University Microfilms.) The author discusses Parker as a "motivic" improviser, categorizing his motives according to size, shape, and frequency of application. Volume 1 contains analysis and commentary and employs Salzerian analytical techniques in its final portion to reveal the larger, formal aspects of Parker's melodies. Volume 2 contains 190 transcriptions of Parker's improvisations.

Shockett, Bernard Irwin. "A Stylistic Study of the Blues as Recorded by Jazz Instrumentalists, 1917—1931." New York University School of Education, 1964. 233 pp. (Microfilm. Ann Arbor: University Microfilms.) The author gives a good historical sketch of tunes with the word "blues" in the title and tabulates information on their forms, meters, tempos, and harmonic frameworks.

Stewart, Milton Lee. "Structural Development in the Jazz Improvisational Technique of Clifford Brown." University of Michigan, 1973. 225 pp. (Microfilm. Ann Arbor: University Microfilms.) This is a study of Brown's improvisational technique based on all four choruses of "I Can Dream, Can't I?" (Prestige 7761).

Discography

The following list of long-playing recordings is divided into those made while Rollins was a sideman and those made under his own name as a leader. The list is nearly complete except for some early issues that are no longer in print or otherwise unavailable. Each entry gives the leader's name (Rollins's name is omitted under his own listings unless it is part of the title), the name of the recording company, the issue number, titles of selections (in parentheses) and the date, location, and personnel, when known. Recordings that have been reissued show the new title(s), if any, and reissue number(s). A complete list of reissues follows.

The following abbreviations are used: t (trumpet), ts (tenor saxophone), as (alto saxophone), bs (bass), p (piano), gt (guitar), dr (drums), trb (trombone), hrn (french horn), vcl (vocal), hp (harp), per (percussion), nyc (New York City), and la (Los Angeles).

1. Recordings as a Sideman

Brown, Clifford, and Roach, Max. *Clifford Brown and Max Roach at Basin Street.* Emarcy MG 36070. (What Is This Thing Called Love?, Love Is a Many Splendored Thing, I'll Remember April, Powell's Prances, Time, The Scene Is Clean, Gertrude's Bounce.) 16—17 February 1956; nyc. Personnel: Rollins, ts; Clifford Brown, t; Richie Powell, p; George Morrow, bs; Max Roach, dr.

Davis, Miles. *Bag's Groove.* Prestige LP 7109. (Airegin, Oleo, But Not for Me, But Not for Me [alternate take], Doxy.) 29 June 1954; Hackensack, N.J. Personnel: Davis, t; Rollins, ts; Horace Silver, p; Percy Heath, bs; Kenny Clarke, dr. Reissued as *Oleo*, Prestige 7847; and *Tallest Trees*, Prestige PR 24012.

———. *Conception.* Prestige LP 7013. (Conception, My Old Flame, Dig, It's Only a Paper Moon, Denial, Out of the Blue, Bluing.) 5 October 1951; nyc. Personnel: Davis, t; Jackie McLean, as; Rollins, ts; Walter Bishop, p; Tommy Potter, bs; Art Blakey, dr. Reissued on Prestige LP 7744 and 24054.

———. *Miles and Horns.* Prestige LP 7025. (Morpheus, Down, Blue Room, Whispering, Tasty Pudding, Willie the Wailer, Floppy, For Adults Only.) 7 January 1951 and 19 February 1953; nyc. Personnel: Davis, t; Bennie Green, trb; Rollins, ts; John Lewis, p; Percy Heath, bs; Roy Haynes, dr. Reissued as *Early Miles*, Prestige LP 7674.

———. *Miles Davis and His Orchestra.* Prestige LP 7044. (Compulsion, The Serpent's Tooth I and II, 'Round Midnight.) 30 January 1953; nyc. Personnel: Davis, t; Charlie Parker and Rollins, ts; Walter Bishop, p; Percy Heath, bs; Philly Joe Jones, dr. Reissued as *Collector's Items*, Prestige 24022.

Dorham, Kenny. *Jazz Contrasts.* Riverside 12—239. (But Beautiful, Falling in Love with Love, I'll Remember April, La Villa, La Rue, My Old Flame.) 21, 27 March 1957; nyc. Personnel; Dorham, t; Rollins, ts; Hank Jones, p; Oscar Pettiford, bs; Betty Glamman, hp; Max Roach, dr.

Farmer, Art. *Early Art.* Prestige LP 177. (Wisteria, Soft Shoe, Confab in Tempo, I'll Take Romance.) 20 January 1954; nyc. Personnel: Farmer, t; Rollins, ts; Horace Silver, p; Percy Heath, bs; Kenny Clarke, dr. Reissued on New Jazz LP 8258.

Gillespie, Dizzy. *Dizzy Gillespie with Sonny Stitt and Sonny Rollins.* Verve 8260. (Wheatleigh Hall, Sumphin' Con Alma, Haute Mon.) 11 December 1957; nyc. Personnel: Gillespie, t; Sonny Stitt and Rollins ts; Ray Bryant, p; Tom Bryant, bs; Charlie Persip, dr. Some selections reissued on Verve 8477 and *Tenor Titan,* Verve 2683 054.

———. *Dizzy Gillespie with Sonny Stitt and Sonny Rollins.* Verve 8262. (The Eternal Triangle, On the Sunny Side of the Street, After Hours, I Know That You Know.) 19 December 1957; nyc. Personnel: same as Verve 8260. Some selections reissued on Verve 8477 and *Tenor Titan,* Verve 2683 054.

Gonzales, Babs. *Babs Gonzales and His Orchestra.* Capitol 57-60000. (Capitolizing, Professor Bop, St. Louis Blues.) 20 January and 27 April 1949; nyc. Personnel: large ensemble with Gonzales, vcl; Rollins, ts.

Johnson, J. J. *Mad Bebop.* Savoy MG 12106. (Don't Blame Me, Audubon, Goof Square, Bee Jay.) February 1949; nyc. Personnel: unknown except for Johnson, trb; Rollins, ts.

Modern Jazz Quartet. *The Modern Jazz Quartet at Music Inn, vol. I.* MGM 1001. (Doxy, Limehouse Blues, I'll Follow My Secret Heart, You Are Too Beautiful, John's Other Theme.) 3 August 1958; Lenox, Mass. Personnel: Milt Jackson, vibraphone; Rollins, ts; John Lewis, p; Percy Heath, bs; Connie Kay, dr. Some selections reissued on *Tenor Titan,* Verve 2683 054.

———. *The Modern Jazz Quartet at Music Inn, vol II.* Atlantic 1299. (Medley [Stardust, I Can't Get Started, Lover Man], Yardbird Suite, Midsömmer, Festival Sketch, Bag's Groove, Night in Tunisia.) 3 August 1958; Lenox, Mass. Personnel: Same as MGM 1001.

———. *The Modern Jazz Quartet with Sonny Rollins.* Prestige LP 7029. (In a Sentimental Mood, The Stopper, Almost Like Being in Love, No Moe.) 7 October 1953; nyc. Personnel: same as Atlantic 1299. Reissued as *First Recordings,* Prestige 7749; all selections reissued on Sonny Rollins, *First Recordings,* Prestige 7856.

Monk, Thelonious. *Thelonious Monk Quintet.* Prestige LP 7053. (Let's Call This, Think of One I, Think of One II, We See, Smoke Gets in Your Eyes, Locomotive, Hackensack.) 11 November 1953 and 11 May 1954; nyc. Personnel: Monk, p; Rollins, ts; Julius Watkins, hrn; Percy Heath, bs; Willie Jones, dr.

———. *Work.* Prestige LP 7169. (I Want to Be Happy, The Way You Look Tonight, More Than You Know, Nutty, Friday the Thirteenth.) 13 November 1953 and 25 October 1954; nyc. Personnel: Monk, p; Rollins, ts; Tommy Potter or Percy Heath, bs; Arthur Taylor, Art Blakey, or Willie Jones, dr; Julius Watkins, hrn. Reissued as the *Genius of Thelonious Monk,* Prestige LP 7656.

Powell, Bud. *The Amazing Bud Powell, vol. I.* Blue Note BLP 1503. (Un Poco Loco, Bouncin' with Bud, Dance of the Infidels, Un Poco Loco [two more takes], 52nd Street Theme, It Could Happen to You, A Night in Tunisia [alternate Master], Wail, Ornithology, Parisian Thoroughfare.) 9 August 1949 and various dates in 1951; nyc. Personnel: Powell, p; Rollins, ts; Fats Navarro, t; Tommy Potter, bs; Roy Haynes or Max Roach, dr.

Roach, Max. *Jazz in 3/4 Time.* Emarcy 36108. (The Most Beautiful Girl in the World, Blues Waltz, Lover, I'll Take Romance, Little Folks, Valse Hot.) 18 and 21 March 1957; nyc. Personnel: Roach, dr; Rollins, ts; Kenny Dorham, t; Ray Bryant, p; George Morrow, bs. Reissued on Trip TLP-5559.

———. *Max Roach Plus Four.* Emarcy MG 36098. (Body and Soul, Ezzthetic, Mister X, Woodyn' You, Doctor Free-zee, Just One of Those Things.) 12 October 1956; nyc. Personnel: same as Emercy 36108.

2. Recordings as a Leader

Alfie. Impulse 9111. (Alfie's Theme, He's Younger Than You Are, Street Runner with Child, Transition Theme, On Impulse, Alfie's Theme Differently.) Released November 1966; London. Personnel: Oliver Nelson Orchestra, Rollins, ts. Reissued on Impulse 9236-2.

Bridge, The. RCA LPM 2527. (Without a Song, Where Are You?, John S., God Bless the Child, You Do Something to Me, The Bridge.) January and February 1962; nyc. Personnel: Rollins, ts; Jim Hall, gt; Bob Cranshaw, bs; Ben Riley or H. T. Saunders, dr. Reissued on RCA 741074/075.

Cutting Edge, The. Milestone M-9059. (The Cutting Edge, To a Wild Rose, First Moves, A House Is Not a Home, Swing Low, Sweet Chariot.) 6 July 1974; Montreux, Switzerland. Personnel: Rollins, ts; Rufus Harley, bagpipes; Masuo, gt; Stanley Cowell, p; Bob Cranshaw, bs; David Lee, dr; Mtume, per.

Don't Ask. Milestone M-9090. (Harlem Boys, The File, Disco Monk, My Ideal, Don't Ask, Tai-Chi, And Then My Love I Found You.) 15—18 May 1979; Berkeley, Calif. Personnel: Rollins, ts; Larry Coryell, gt; Mark Soskin, p; Jerome Harris, bs; Al Foster, dr; Bill Summers, per.

Don't Stop the Carnival. Milestone M-55005. (Don't Stop the Carnival, Silver City, Autumn Nocturne, Camel, Nobody Else But Me, Non-Cents, A Child's Prayer, President Hayes, Sais.) 14—15 April 1978; San Francisco. Personnel: Rollins, ts; Donald Byrd, t; Mark Soskin, p; Aurell Ray, gt; Jerry Harris, bs; Tony Williams, dr.

East Broadway Run Down. Impulse S-9121. (East Broadway Run Down, We Kiss in a Shadow, Blessing in Disguise.) 9 May 1966; nyc. Personnel: Rollins, ts; Freddie Hubbard, t; Jimmy Garrison, bs; Elvin Jones, dr.

Easy Living. Milestone M-9080. (Isn't She Lovely, Down the Line, My One and Only Love, Arroz con Pollo, Easy Living, Hear What I'm Saying.) 3—6 August 1977; Berkeley, Calif. Personnel: Rollins, ts; George Duke, keyboards; Charles Icarus Johnson, gt; Paul Jackson, bs; Tony Williams, dr.

Freedom Suite. Riverside RLP 12—258. (Freedom Suite, Someday I'll Find You, Shadow Waltz, 'Til There Was You [Two Takes] Will You Still Be

Mine?) 11 February and 7 March 1958; nyc. Personnel: Rollins, ts; Oscar Pettiford, bs; Max Roach, dr. Reissued on *Freedom Suite Plus*, Milestone 47007.

Graz 1963 Concert. Jazz Connoisseur JC-108. (Title Unknown, Title Unknown [Love Walked In], Poinciana.) 1963; Graz, Austria. Personnel: Rollins, ts; Jimmy Merit, bs; Max Roach, dr.

Horn Culture. Milestone M-9051. (Pictures in the Reflection of a Golden Horn, Sais, Notes for Eddie, God Bless the Child, Love Man, Good Morning Heartache.) 4 and 6 July 1973; Berkeley, Calif. Personnel: Rollins, ts; Walter Davis, p; Masuo, gt; Bob Cranshaw, bs; David Lee, dr; Mtume, per.

Love at First Sight. Milestone M-9098. (Little Lu, The Dream That We Fell Out Of, Strode Rode, The Very Thought of You, Caress, Double Feature.) 9—12 May 1980; Berkeley, Calif. and nyc, Personnel: Rollins, ts; George Duke, keyboards; Stanley Clarke, bs; Al Foster, dr; Bill Summers, per.

Milestone Jazzstars. Milestone M-55006. (The Cutting Edge, N. O. Blues, Nubia, Don't Stop the Carnival, In a Sentimental Mood, Alone Together, Continuum, Willow Weep for Me, A Little Pianissimo.) Fall 1978, Rollins, ts; McCoy Tyner, p; Ron Carter, bs; Al Foster, dr.

More from the Vanguard. Blue Note BN-LA475-H2. (I've Got You under My Skin, Night in Tunisia, What Is This Thing Called Love? Softly as a Morning Sunrise, Four, Woodyn' You, All the Things You Are, Get Happy, I'll Remember April, Get Happy [alternate version].) 3 November 1957; nyc. Personnel: Rollins, ts; Dave Bailey or Wilbur Ware, bs; Pete LaRocca or Elvin Jones, dr.

Moving Out. Prestige LP 7058. (Moving Out, Swinging for Bunny, Silk 'n Satin, Solid, More Than You Know.) 18 August 1954; nyc. Personnel: Rollins, ts; Kenny Dorham, t; Elmo Hope or Thelonious Monk, p; Percy Heath or Tommy Potter, bs; Art Blakey or Art Taylor, dr. Reissued as *Jazz Classics*, Prestige 7433.

Newk's Time. Blue Note BLP 4001. (Tune Up, Asiatic Raes, Wonderful, Wonderful, The Surrey with the Fringe on Top, Blues for Philly, Namely You.) 28 September 1958; nyc. Personnel: Rollins, ts; Wynton Kelly, p; Doug Watkins, bs; Philly Joe Jones, dr. Some selections reissued on Blue Note BN-LA 401-H2.

Night at the Village Vanguard. Blue Note BLP 1581. (Sonnymoon for Two, Old Devil Moon, Softly as in a Morning Sunrise, Shriver's Row, I Can't Get Started, A Night in Tunisia.) 3 November 1957; nyc. Personnel: Rollins, ts; Dave Bailey or Wilbur Ware, bs; Pete LaRocca or Elvin Jones, dr. Some selections appear on *More from the Vanguard*, Blue Note BN-LA 475-H2.

Now's the Time. RCA LPM-2927. (Now's the Time, Blue 'n' Boogie, I Remember Clifford, Fifty-Second Street Theme, St. Thomas, 'Round Midnight, Afternoon in Paris, Four.) 1963; nyc. Personnel: Rollins, ts; Bob Cranshaw, bs; Roy McCurdy, dr.

Nucleus. Milestone M-9064. (Lucille, Gwaligo, Are You Ready?, Azalea, Newkleus, Cosmet, My Reverie.) 2—5 September 1975; Berkeley, Calif. Personnel: Rollins and Bennie Maupin, ts; Raul de Souza, trb; George Duke, keyboards; David Amaro and Black Bird, gt; Bob Cranshaw, Chuck Rainey, bs; Roy McCurdy, Eddie Moore, dr; Mtume, per.

On Impulse. Impulse A-91. (On Green Dolphin Street, Everything Happens to Me, Hold 'Em Joe, Blue Room, Three Little Words.) 8 July 1965; nyc. Personnel: Rollins, ts; Jimmy Garrison, bs; Elvin Jones, dr. Reissued as *Green Dolphin Street*, Quintessence QJ-25181.

Our Man in Jazz. RCA LPM-2612. (Oleo, Dearly Beloved, Doxy.) July 1962; nyc. Personnel: Rollins, ts; Don Cherry, t; Bob Cranshaw, bs; Billy Higgins, dr. Reissued as *Sonny Rollins*, vol. 4, RCA 741091/092.

Saxophone Colossus. Prestige LP 7079. (You Don't Know What Love Is, St. Thomas, Strode Rode, Blue Seven, Moritat). 22 June 1956; nyc. Personnel: Rollins, ts; Tommy Flannagan, p; Doug Watkins, bs; Max Roach, dr. Reissued on *Saxophone Colossus and More*, Prestige P-24050.

Sonny and the Stars. Prestige LP 7029. (I Know, Newk's Fadeaway, Time on My Hands, Mambo Bounce, This Love of Mine, Shadrack, Slow Boat to China, With a Song in My Heart, Scoops.) 17 January and 17 December 1951; nyc. Personnel: Rollins, ts; Miles Davis, Kenny Drew, p; Percy Heath, bs; Roy Haynes, Art Blakey, dr. Reissued on *First Recordings*, Prestige 7856; also Prestige 7269.

Sonny Meets Hawk. RCA LPM-2712. (Yesterdays, All the Things You Are, Summertime, Just Friends, Lover Man, At McKies.) 15 and 18 July 1963; nyc. Personnel: Rollins and Coleman Hawkins, ts; Paul Bley, p; Henry Grimes, Bob Cranshaw, bs; Roy McCurdy, dr. Reissued as *Sonny Rollins*, vol. 2, RCA 741074/075.

Sonny Rollins. Period LP 1204. (Sunny Moon for Two, Like Someone in Love, Theme from Tchaikovsky's Symphony Pathetique, Lust for Life, I Got It Thad, Ballad Medley.) 4 November 1957; nyc. Personnel: Rollins, ts; Thad Jones, t; Jimmy Cleveland, trb; Gil Coggins, p; Wendall Marshall, bs; Kenny Dennis, dr. Reissued as *Sonny Rollins*, Archive FS-220.

Sonny Rollins and the Big Brass. Verve 8430. (Grand Street, Far Out East, Who Cares?, Love Is a Simple Thing, What's My Name?, If You Were the Only Girl in the World, Manhattan, Body and Soul.) 10—11 July 1958; nyc. Personnel: Rollins, ts; Nat Adderley, Clark Terry, Reunald Jones, Ernie Royal, t; Billy Byers, Jimmy Cleveland, Frank Rehak, trb; Don Butterfield, tuba; Dick Katz, p; Rene Thomas, gt; Henry Grimes, bs; Roy Haynes, dr. Some selections reissued on *Tenor Titan*, Verve 2683 054.

Sonny Rollins and the Contemporary Leaders. Contemporary C-3564. (Alone Together, I've Told Every Little Star, Rock-A-Bye Your Baby, How High the Moon, You, I've Found a New Baby, In the Chapel in the Moonlight, The Song Is You.) 20 and 22 October 1958; la. Personnel; Rollins, ts; Hampton Hawes, p; Barney Kessel, gt; Vic Feldman, vibes;, Leroy Vinnegar, bs; Shelly Manne, dr.

Sonny Rollins' Next Album. Milestone MSP-9042. (Playin' in the Yard, Poinciana, The Everywhere Calypso, Keep Hold of Yourself, Skylark.) July 1972; nyc. Personnel: Rollins, ts; George Cables, keyboards; Bob Cranshaw, bs; Jack DeJohnette or David Lee, dr; Arthur Jenkins, per.

Sonny Rollins Plays for Bird. Prestige 7095. (I've Grown Accustomed to Your Face, Kids Know, Bird Medley [I Remember You, Star Eyes, My Melancholy Baby, They Can't Take That Away from Me, Old Folks, Just Friends, My Little Suede Shoes].) 5 October 1956; nyc. Personnel: Rollins, ts;

Kenny Dorham, t; Wade Legge, p; George Morrow, bs; Max Roach, dr. Some selections reissued on *Saxophone Colossus and More*, Prestige P-24050.

Sonny Rollins Plus Four. Prestige 7038. (I Feel a Song Coming On, Pent-Up House, Valse Hot, Kiss and Run, Count Your Blessings.) 22 March 1956; nyc. Personnel: Rollins, ts; Clifford Brown, t; Richie Powell, p; George Morrow, b; Max Roach, dr. Reissued as *Three Giants*, Prestige 7821; some selections reissued on *Saxophone Colossus and More*, Prestige P-24050.

Sonny Rollins: Volume I. Blue Note BLP 1542. (Decision, Plain Jane, Blues-note, How Are Things in Glocca Morra?, Sonnysphere.) 16 December 1956; nyc. Personnel: Rollins, ts; Donald Byrd, t; Wynton Kelly, p; Gene Ramey, bs; Max Roach, dr. Most selections are reissued on Blue Note BN-LA 401—H2.

Sonny Rollins: Volume II. Blue Note BLP 1558. (Why Don't I?, Wail March, Misterioso, Reflections, You Stepped Out of a Dream, Poor Butterfly.) 14 April 1957; nyc. Personnel: Rollins, ts; J. J. Johnson, trb; Horace Silver and Thelonious Monk, p; Paul Chambers, bs; Art Blakey, dr. Most selections are reissued on Blue Note BN-LA 401-H2.

Sound of Sonny, The. Riverside RLP-12-241. (The Last Time I Saw Paris, Just in Time, Toot, Toot, Tootsie, What Is There to Say?, Dearly Beloved, Everytime We Say Goodbye, Cutie, It Could Happen to You, Mangoes.) 11, 12, and 19 June 1957; nyc. Personnel: Rollins, ts; Sonny Clark, p; Percy Heath, or Paul Chambers, bs; Roy Haynes, dr. Reissued on *The Freedom Suite Plus*, Milestone 47007.

Standard Sonny Rollins, The. RCA LPM-3355. (Autumn Nocturne, Night and Day, Love Letters, My One and Only Love, Three Little Words, Travelin' Light, I'll Be Seeing You, My Ship, It Could Happen to You, Long Ago and Far Away.) 1965; nyc. Personnel: Rollins, ts; Herbie Hancock, p; Jim Hall, gt; Bob Cranshaw, Dave Izenzon, Teddie Smith, bs; Mickey Roker, Stu Martin, dr.

Stuttgart 1963 Concert. Jazz Connoisseur JC-106. (52nd Street Theme, On Green Dolphin Street, Sonnymoon for Two.) 1963; Stuttgart, W. Germany. Personnel: Rollins, ts; Don Cherry, t; Henry Grimes, bs; Billy Higgins, dr.

Tenor Madness. Prestige LP 7047. (Reverie, The Most Beautiful Girl in the World, Paul's Pal, When Your Lover Has Gone, Tenor Madness.) 24 May 1956; nyc. Personnel: Rollins and John Coltrane, ts; Red Garland, p; Paul Chambers, bs; Philly Joe Jones, dr. Some of these reissued on *Taking Care of Business*, Prestige 24082; also Prestige 24004.

There Will Never Be Another You. Impulse IA-9349. (On Green Dolphin Street, Three Little Words, Mademoiselle de Paris, To a Wild Rose, There Will Never Be Another You). 17 June 1965; nyc. Personnel: Rollins, ts; Tommy Flanagan, p; Bob Cranshaw, bs; Billy Higgins and Mickey Roker, dr.

Tour de Force. Prestige 7126. (B. Swift, My Ideal, Two Different Worlds, Ee ah, B. Quick.) 7 December 1956; nyc. Personnel: Rollins, ts; Kenny Drew, p; George Morrow, bs; Max Roach, dr; Earl Coleman, vcl. Most selections are reissued on *Sonny Boy*, Prestige LP 7207.

Way I Feel, The. Milestone M-9074. (Island Lady, Asfrantation Woogie, Love Reborn, Happy Feel, Shout It Out, The Way I Feel About You, Charm

Baby.) August and October 1976; la. Personnel: Rollins, ts; Patrice
Rushen, keyboards; Lee Ritenour, gt; Alex Blake, Charles Meeks, bs; Billy
Cobham, dr; Bill Summers, per.

Way Out West. Contemporary C-3530. (Solitude, Wagon Wheels, Way Out
West, No Greater Love, I'm an Old Cowhand, Come, Gone.) 7 March 1957;
la. Personnel: Rollins, ts; Ray Brown, bs; Shelly Manne, dr.

What's New? RCA LPM-2572. (Don't Stop the Carnival, Jungoso, Bluesongo,
Brownskin Girl, You Are My Lucky Star, I Could Write a Book, There Will
Never Be Another You.) 5 April and 14 May 1962; nyc. Personnel: Rollins,
ts; Don Cherry, cornet; Jim Hall, gt; Bob Cranshaw, Henry Grimes, bs; Ben
Riley, Billy Higgins, dr; Willy Rodriguez, Dennis Charles, Frank Charles,
Dandido Camero, per. Reissued as *Pure Gold*, RCA ANL1-2809 and on
RCA 74109/092.

Worktime. Prestige LP 7246. (There's No Business Like Show Business,
Paradox, Raincheck, There Are Such Things, It's Alright with Me). 2
December 1955; nyc. Personnel: Rollins, ts; Ray Bryant, p; George
Morrow, bs; Max Roach, dr. Reissued as Prestige LP 7750; some on *Taking
Care of Business*, Prestige P-24082.

3. Reissues

Davis, Miles. *Collector's Items.* Prestige 24022. See *Miles Davis and His Orchestra.*

——. *Early Miles.* Prestige LP 7674. See *Miles and Horns.*

——. *Oleo.* Prestige LP 7847. See *Bag's Groove.*

——. *Tallest Trees.* Prestige PR 24012. See *Bag's Groove.*

Gillespie, Dizzy. *Dizzy Gillespie with Sonny Stitt and Sonny Rollins.* Verve
8477. See Verve 8260.

Modern Jazz Quartet, The. *First Recordings.* Prestige LP 7749. See *The
Modern Jazz Quartet with Sonny Rollins.*

Monk, Thelonious. *The Genius of Thelonious Monk.* Prestige LP 7656. See
Work.

Rollins, Sonny. *First Recordings.* Prestige LP 7856. See *The Modern Jazz
Quartet with Sonny Rollins* and *Sonny and the Stars.*

——. *Freedom Suite Plus.* Milestone 47007. See the *Freedom Suite* and *The
Sound of Sonny.*

——. *Green Dolphin Street.* Quintessence QJ-25181. See *On Impulse.*

——. *Jazz Classics.* Prestige LP 7433. See *Moving Out.*

——. *Pure Gold.* RCA ANL1-2809. See *What's New?*

——. *Reevaluation: The Impulse Years.* Impulse AS-9236-2. See *East Broadway Run Down* and *Alfie.*

——. *Saxophone Colossus and More.* Prestige P-24050. See *Saxophone
Colossus, Sonny Rollins Plays for Bird,* and *Sonny Rollins Plus Four.*

——. *Sonny Boy.* Prestige LP 7207. See *Tour de Force.*

——. *Sonny Rollins.* Prestige 24004. See *Tenor Madness Saxophone Colossus, Sonny and the Stars,* and *Sonny Rollins Plus Four.*

——. *Sonny Rollins.* Archive of Folk Music FS-220. See *Sonny Rollins,* Period
LP 1204.

————. *Sonny Rollins,* Blue Note BN-LA401-H2. See *Sonny Rollins, Vol. I* and *II* and *Newk's Time.*

————. *Sonny Rollins, Volumes 1 and 2.* RCA 741074/075 See *The Bridge* and *Sonny Meets Hawk.*

————. *Sonny Rollins, Volumes 3 and 4.* RCA 74109/092. See *What's New?* and *Our Man in Jazz.*

————. *Taking Care of Business.* Prestige P-24082. See *Worktime, Sonny Boy,* and *Tenor Madness.*

————. *Tenor Titan.* Verve 2683 054. See *Dizzy Gillespie with Sonny Stitt and Sonny Rollins, Sonny Rollins and the Big Brass* and *The Modern Jazz Quartet at Music Inn, Vol. I.*

————. *Three Giants.* Prestige LP 7821. See *Sonny Rollins Plus Four.*

Index